130
French Inns
and Small Hotels

Filipacchi Publishing
1633 Broadway
New York, NY 10019

Translated from French by Simon Pleasance and Fronza Woods
Copyedited by Samantha Berman

ISBN: 2 85018 637 6

Color separation: Quadrilaser
Printed and bound in C.E.E.

Marie-Dominique Perrin

130 French Inns and Small Hotels

Delightful Places Starting at $40

Photographs by Christophe Valentin

TRAVEL HOLIDAY

filipacchi publishing

Contents

Southeast p.8

Southwest p.58

Centre-Auvergne p.92

West and North p.114

East p.140

Index by "départements" p.154

Index by price range p.156

SAINT-AMAND-MONTROND
LOUHANS
LONS-LE-SAUNIER
LA CHATRE
MOULINS
CHAROLLES
SAINT-CLAUDE
Lac Léman
MONTLUÇON
MACON
BOURG-EN-BRESSE
GEX
THONON-LES-BAINS
GUERET
NANTUA
VICHY
ROANNE
VILLEFRANCHE-SUR-SAONE
BONNEVILLE
SAINT-JULIEN-EN-GENEVOIS
Les Carroz d'Arâches
AUVERGNE
ANNECY
Chamonix
RIOM
Le Grand-Bornand
Manigod
AUBUSSON
THIERS
BELLEY
CLERMONT-FERRAND
LYON
RHONE-ALPES
ALBERTVILLE
LIMOUSIN
CHAMBERY
MONTBRISON
USSEL
ISSOIRE
AMBERT
VIENNE
LA TOUR-DU-PIN
St-Martin-de-Belleville
SAINT-ETIENNE
SAINT-JEAN-DE-MAURIENNE
TULLE
BRIOUDE
Châtillon-St-Jean
MAURIAC
YSSINGEAUX
TOURNON
GRENOBLE
BRIVE-LA-GAILLARDE
SAINT-FLOUR
LE PUY-EN-VELAY
AURILLAC
VALENCE
BRIANÇON
DIE
Pô
PRIVAS
Cliousclat
GOURDON
Laguiole
GAP
FIGEAC
Entraygues
MENDE
LARGENTIERE
Grignan
Labastide-de-Virac
Belcastel
BARCELONNETTE
CAHORS
RODEZ
Beaulieu
Nyons
Colonzelle
Enchastrayes
FLORAC
VILLEFRANCHE-DE-ROUERGUE
DIGNE-LES-BAINS
Beaumont-du-Ventoux
Ribaute-les-Tavernes
ALES
CARPENTRAS
Mazan
Millau
St-Maximin
FORCALQUIER
AVIGNON
LE VIGAN
CASTELLANE
APT
Tarascon
Ménerbes
PROVENCE-ALPES-COTE D'AZUR
Vence
MONACO
NIMES
ALBI
GRASSE
NICE
St-Etienne-du-Grès
Eygalières
Haut-de-Cagnes
LODEVE
Golfe-Juan-Vallauris
Le Puy-Ste-Réparade
MONTPELLIER
Arles
Antibes
TOULOUSE
CASTRES
St-Antonin-s-Bayon
DRAGUIGNAN
AIX-EN-PROVENCE
ISTRES
LANGUEDOC-
MARSEILLE
BRIGNOLES
La Celle
Erbalunga
BEZIERS
Cassis
Bormes-les-Mimosas
CARCASSONNE
NARBONNE
TOULON
BASTIA
Fajac-en-Val
Pigna
Calvi
HAUTE
PAMIERS
LIMOUX
Cervione
CORTE
Durban
FOIX
Cascastel
CORSE
ROUSSILLON
CORSE
Torreilles
Perpignan
Alénya
DU
Corneilla-del-Vercol
AJACCIO
PRADES
SUD
CERET
0
50
100 km
SARTENE

Southeast

Le Mas Samarcande
06220 Golfe-Juan-Vallauris.

Le Bosquet
06160 Antibes-Juan-les-Pins.

La Villa Estelle
06800 Haut-de-Cagnes.

La Roseraie
06140 Vence.

La Bastide rose
83230 Bormes-les-Mimosas.

La Grande Maison
83230 Bormes-les-Mimosas.

Hostellerie de l'Abbaye de La Celle
83170 La Celle.

Le Jardin d'Emile
13260 Cassis.

Le Mas dou Pastre
13810 Eygalières.

Aux Deux Sœurs
13210 Saint-Etienne-du-Grès.

Le Calendal
13200 Arles.

La Maison d'Hôtes
13150 Tarascon.

Le Mas des Arnajons
13610 Le Puy-Sainte-Réparade.

La Haute-Terre
13100 Saint-Antonin-sur-Bayon.

La Maison
84340 Beaumont-du-Ventoux.

La Grange de Jusalem
84380 Mazan.

La Bastide de Marie
84560 Ménerbes.

La Treille muscate
26270 Cliousclat.

Une Autre Maison
26110 Nyons.

La Maison Forte de Clérivaux
26750 Châtillon-Saint-Jean.

La Maison de Soize
26230 Colonzelle.

Le Clair de Plume
26230 Grignan.

La Santoline
07460 Beaulieu.

Le Couradou
07150 Labastide-de-Virac.

Le Vivier
04400 Enchastrayes.

La Crémerie du Glacier
74400 Chamonix.

Les Servages
74300 Les Carroz d'Arâches.

L'Hôtel des Cimes
74450 Le Grand-Bornand.

Le Chalet-hôtel de la Croix-Fry
74230 Manigod.

Hôtel Saint-Martin
73440 Saint-Martin-de-Belleville.

Le Château de Saint-Maximin
30700 Saint-Maximin.

Le Mas de l'Amandier
30720 Ribaute-les-Tavernes.

Le Mas Bazan
66200 Alénya.

Laurence Jonquères d'Oriola
66200 Corneilla-del-Vercol.

La Vieille Demeure
66440 Torreilles.

La Villa Duflot
66000 Perpignan.

Le Grand Guilhem
11360 Cascastel.

Le Domaine du Haut-Gléon
11360 Durban.

La Mignoterie
11220 Fajac-en-Val

La Méjanassère
12140 Entraygues.

La Ferme de Moulhac
12210 Laguiole.

L'Hôtel du Vieux-Pont
12390 Belcastel.

La Musardière
12100 Millau.

La Villa Calvi
20260 Calvi.

La Signoria
20260 Calvi.

La Casa Musicale
20220 Pigna.

La Casa Corsa
20221 Cervione.

Castel Brando
20222 Erbalunga.

Le Mas Samarcande

Mr. and Mrs. Diot, 138, bd de Super-Cannes, 06220 Golfe-Juan-Vallauris.
Tel/fax: 011 33 4 93 63 97 73. www.stpaulweb.com/samarcande mireille.diot@wanadoo.fr

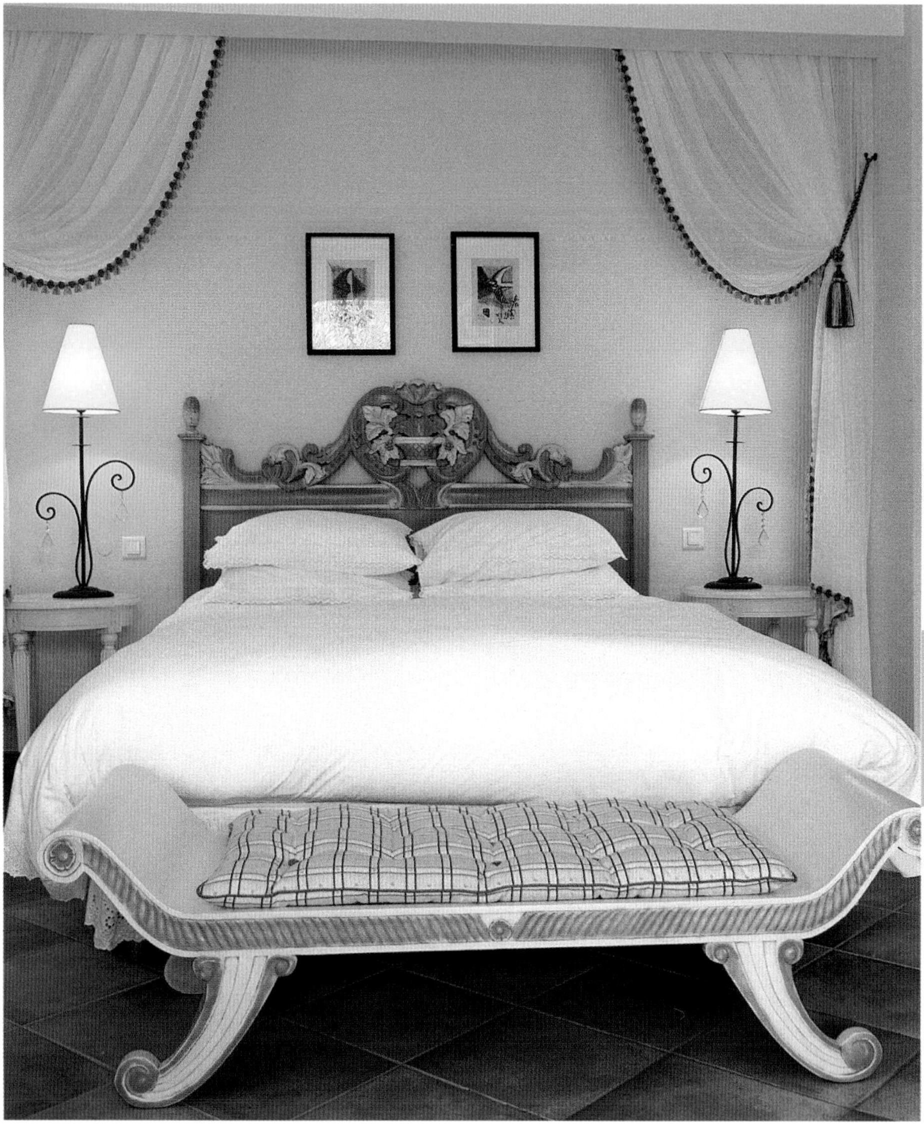

Pierre Diot's profession as a photographer has given him a taste for beautiful things and the Provençal art of living. Accordingly, somewhere between the warmth of a guest house and the independence of a small hotel, he offers five divine rooms in a farmhouse on a hillside landscaped with Mediterranean shrubbery. Beneath its canopy imported from Asia, the "Samarcande" room, after which the house is named, is an interplay on shades of brown and beige. It has a Caribbean-Colonial style, while "Lérins" and "Porquerolles" have a maritime feel, with powder blues and sunny brick reds. "Manosque" is done up in vermilion Jouy and cobalt, and opens onto a small garden-cum-terrace enhanced by oleander in large pots. The bathrooms, with their indirect lights in polished glass, are gentle on the eyes, and for sweet dreams, just before bedtime you'll find a marzipan or orange candy on your bedside table.

■ 5 rooms: $110.
■ Breakfast included.
■ Open year round.

Le Bosquet

Mr. and Mrs. Aussel, 14, chemin des Sables, 06160 Antibes-Juan-les-Pins.
Tel/fax: 011 33 4 93 67 32 29. lebosquet@infonie.fr

A pretty villa set back on the Chemin des Sables, this 17th and 18th century home was originally a country cottage, enlarged by an erstwhile pirate hailing from Guérande who married a young woman from the Antibes bourgeoisie. Behind the inn's tea-rose façade, set in the midst of palm trees, light filters through closed Venetian blinds, keeping the rooms cool. Sisal carpets cover Provençal floor tiles. A bamboo-print patchwork covers the "Blue" room, creating a soft atmosphere. Azure-hued Baroque sets the tone for the "Yellow" room around an Italian wrought iron bed, a chaise longue, painted furniture, and ancestral portraits. And for your siesta in the garden, a hammock is slung between the huge branches of a bay tree.

- 3 rooms: $70–$100.
- Breakfast included.
- Closed from November 15 to December 15.

La Roseraie

Monica and Maurice Garnier, 51, avenue Henri-Giraud, 06140 Vence.
Tel: 011 33 4 93 58 02 20. Fax: 011 33 4 93 58 99 31.

Palm and banana trees sweep the air with their broad leaves. Magnolia and eucalyptus spread their fragrance over a bed of roses encircling the swimming pool. The centuries-old tradition of vacationing which used to define this idyllic site has given way to a small hotel matching its Provençal hues with old-fashioned objects discovered in flea markets. Innkeepers Maurice and Monica Garnier have added a personal touch to the rooms here with their walls painted in sunny colors, 18th century doors, and original curtain rods made by a local blacksmith. They have also placed wicker chests, bursting with roses, about on landings, and in the rooms they've put old typewriters, conjuring simpler times. In in the bathrooms, *azulejos* and tiles from Salernes capture the appropriate spirit.

- 18 rooms: $70–$165.
- Breakfast: $15.
- Mini-bar in each room.
- Pool.
- Closed from November 15 to February 15.

La Villa Estelle

Estelle Réale, 5, montée de la Bourgade, 06800 Haut-de-Cagnes.
Tel: 011 33 4 92 02 89 83. Fax: 011 33 4 92 02 88 28. www.villa-estelle.com

Estelle Réale admits that when she bought this splendid residence above Cagnes, two things won her over: the large terrace with its neo-Roman columns basking in sunlight, surveying the blue square of the Mediterranean in the distance; and the huge lock, which, Sesame-like, opened the door of this old tavern which over the years had received guests as notable as Maharani of Boroda, Foujita, and Cocteau. The straw-colored façade now has plum-colored shutters, adding coolness to alcoves with shades of dogrose, dried hay, red ochre, and azure.

Estelle is extremely gifted in the art of mixing: natural fabrics and velvet curtains; sources of colonial inspiration and bathrooms in marble resin; hats from Nice and generous 18th century sofas. In the end, you get a fine lesson in harmony between Baroque and Art Deco.

- 6 rooms and 1 suite: $150–$230.
- Breakfast: $12–$20.
- Open year round.

Var

La Bastide rose

Isabelle and Didier Lardaud, 464, chemin du Patelin, 83230 Bormes-les-Mimosas.
Tel: 011 33 4 94 71 35 77. Fax: 011 33 4 94 71 35 88. bastide.rose@wanadoo.fr

Pink ochre walls set the scene for this house located only five minutes from the sea. The light filtering through the closed shutters holds onto an Oriental atmosphere. It strikes the sofa cushions scented with essential oils, brings out the velvety texture of a fireplace, enhances the saffron walls of one bedroom, and the orange-colored drapes of another. At La Bastide Rose, the Provençal countryside combines with a dreamlike Orient in every room of the house.

- 3 rooms: $90–$165.
- 1 suite, sleeps 3: starting at $120.
- Breakfast included.
- Pool.
- Spa.
- Closed from September 30 to March 31.

La Grande Maison

Var

Laurance Lapinet, Domaine des Campaux, RN 98 - Forêt du Dom, 83230 Bormes-les-Mimosas.
Tel: 011 33 4 94 49 55 40. Fax: 011 33 4 94 49 55 23.

This is a slightly Bohemian house set in a winegrowing estate on the Var coast. When it's siesta time, you head for the freshness of the bedrooms, walking barefoot on terra-cotta floors brightened by colorful kilims and flower-patterned rugs. The spirit of Provence imbues walls and fabric alike, with pine furniture and bouquets of dried flowers in rooms done up in colors such as sky, peach, warm sand, and oleander. Tiles from Salernes, a hallmark of the Var, are used in the decoration of each bathroom. Old postcards, captured in wooden frames, offer a nostalgic vision of this region. And you can taste its specialties every night at innkeeper Laurance Lapinet's table.

- 3 rooms and 2 suites: $90–$130.
- Breakfast: $10.
- Meals: $30.
- Open year round.

Hostellerie de l'Abbaye de La Celle

Place du Général de Gaulle, 83170 La Celle. **Tel: 011 33 4 98 05 14 14.**
Fax: 011 33 4 98 05 14 15. www.abbaye-celle.com contact@abbaye-celle.com

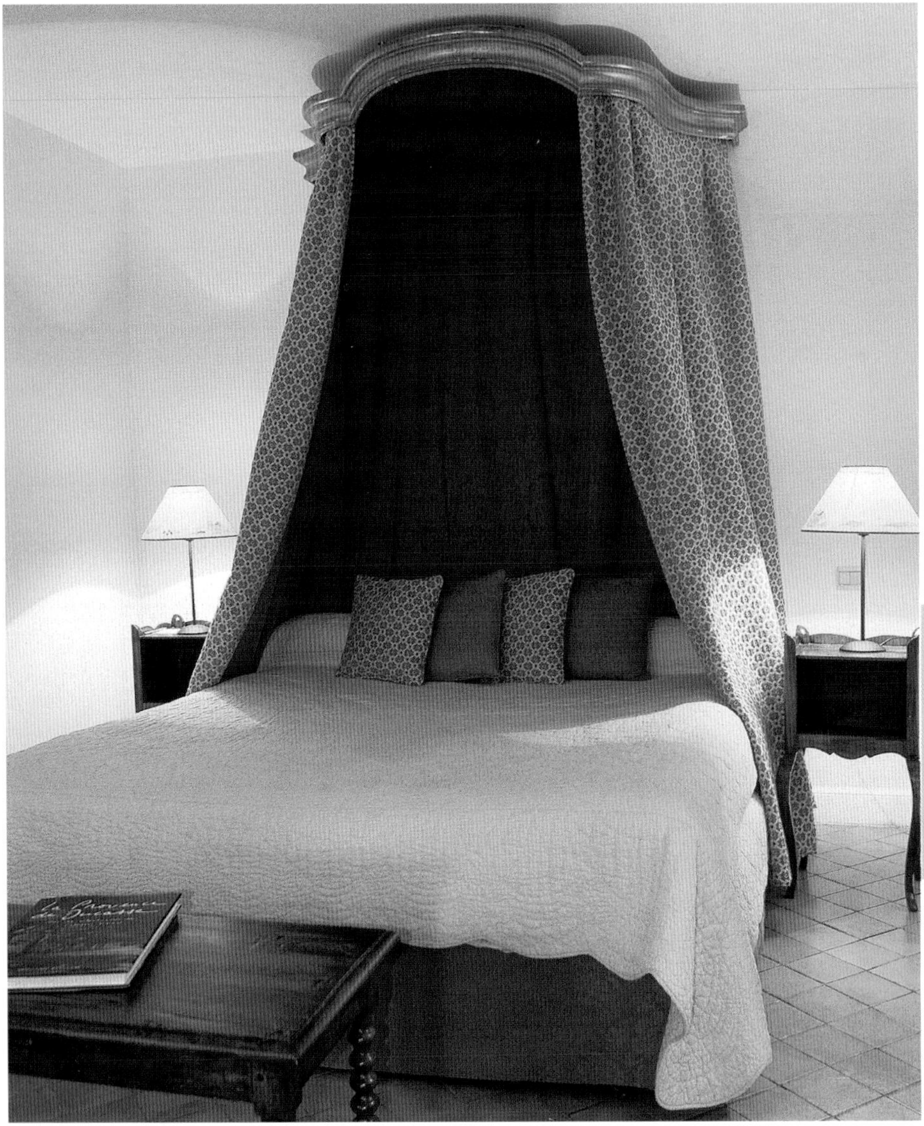

Nuns deemed too naughty were asked to move out of this 12th century chapter house which Alain Ducasse has renovated with a thoroughly Cistercian sobriety. Now, travelers come to make the most of the age-old hospitality of this abbey hemmed in by Var vineyards. When the dawn mists break up and the curtain of cypress trees, the vegetable garden, and the forest come into view, it's a must to take a country breakfast on the terrace furnished with pretty theater seats, or beneath the arcades of branches in the garden. Later, eat dinner in the luminous white dining room, offset by carved woodwork retrieved from a ship. Amber, honey, and candied chestnut lights spread relaxing tones through the ten bedrooms in this hostelry and its Beguine convent. The most mythical of all is the room used, in his day, by General de Gaulle, where leather luggage and boots still seem to be waitingfor him near a sepia-colored screen.

- 9 rooms and 1 suite: $200–$270.
- Breakfast: $15.
- Menus: $35 and $60.
- Pool.
- Closed from January 7 to February 7.

Le Jardin d'Emile

Plage du Bestouan, 13260 Cassis. **Tel: 011 33 4 42 01 80 55.**
Fax: 011 33 4 42 01 80 70. provence@jardindemile.fr

This inn sports a delightful garden planted beneath soaring umbrella pines on the edge of Bestouan beach. Nearby, tables with ochre-and saffron-striped cloths beckon gourmets who will feast on sun-blessed fare. Behind its sienna façade, the cottage houses seven small rooms with gingerbread-colored walls and terra-cotta floors. Quilted bedspreads and lavender, mauve, and sunflower throws enhance the rooms, and half-closed Venetian blinds invite you to take a quick siesta before dinner—slip into the cool linen sheets and listen to the lapping of the sea close by.

- 7 rooms: $65–$110.
- Breakfast: $10.
- Meals: starting at $30.
- Closed from November 15 to November 30 and in January.

Le Mas dou Pastre

Route d'Orgon, 13810 Eygalières. **Tel: 011 33 4 90 95 92 61.**
Fax: 011 33 4 90 90 61 75. www.alpilles.com

This old family house has, little by little, been transformed into a charming hotel with a dozen indisputably Provence-style rooms. Cicadas have set up shop in a room named after them, and no one would dream of getting rid of them. The "Clair de Lune" room softens the night with slate hues while the "Provençales" room is done in a gentle almond-green color. Red currant and sunflower are the dominant hues in "Quatre Saisons." In "La Belle Etoile," you'll sleep beneath fluttering muslin. On an even more feminine note, "Sous la treille" has pink quilted bedspreads and "La Tonnelle" is covered in ivy stenciling. And then in the garden, you'll find two genuine gypsy caravans painted firecracker red: One is equipped with a tiled bathroom, the other with the bathtub cast in copper—but both eagerly await weekend bohemian guests.

- 12 rooms and caravans: $65–$150.
- 1 suite for 4 people: $190.
- Breakfast: $12.
- Pool.
- Open year round.

Aux Deux Sœurs

Carolyn Wood, le Vieux Chemin d'Arles, 13210 Saint-Etienne-du-Grès.
Tel: 011 33 4 90 49 10 18. Fax: 011 33 4 90 49 10 30. ads.wood.gites@infonie.fr

Sunny decor is the hallmark of this large 19th century house purchased by Carolyn Wood, who had come bargain hunting in the Alpilles for bits and pieces for her London restaurant. In the end she decided to stay. Fabrics by one of Britain's most gifted designers brighten up windows and beds with gold, plum, and lime. Posters of Nîmes bullfights signed by the artists adorn the walls. Splendid linen cupboards fill the entrance hall, while an old Provençal door, turned into a low table, welcomes the international clientele which frequents this hotel. Every room has a TV and—something not so common—a well-stocked video library with films in several languages.

- 2 rooms: $100-$120.
- 1 suite: $150.
- 1 cottage, sleeps 3: $475–$620 for a week.
- 1 cottage, sleeps 5: $620– $1,200 for a week.
- Breakfast included.
- Meals: $35.
- Pool.
- Open year round.

Le Calendal

5, rue Porte de Laure, 13200 Arles. **Tel: 011 33 4 90 96 11 89.**
Fax: 011 33 4 90 96 05 84. www.lecalendal.com contact@lecalendal.com

This hotel is a real haven of peace in the heart of old Arles, between the Ancient Theater and the Amphitheater. In other words, it's a place in the thick of things, yet you can quietly experience a Roman ambience. It all starts on the cool Mediterranean patio, where a 400-year-old nettletree shades the contemporary wrought iron garden furniture. Behind its olive-green shutters, Le Calendal, so-named after a Frédéric Mistral hero, boasts 38 rooms decorated in a range of colors matching the stencils and local furnishings in them. "Tamaris," with its lemon-and-blue furniture, feels fresh and clean. "Figuier," in its bouquet of pinks, wins female approval. "Pomme d'amour/Love Apple" is wonderful for a solo traveler. And "Saladelle," with its rooftop terrace bordered in Roman tiles, offers sunbathing in perfect peace and quiet, plus views of the Montmajour abbey off in the distance.

- 38 rooms and suites: $45–$100.
- Breakfast: $8.
- Closed from July 7 to July 27.

La Maison d'Hôtes

24, rue du Château, 13150 Tarascon. **Tel: 011 33 4 90 91 09 99.**
Fax: 011 33 4 90 91 10 33. ylaraison@wanadoo.fr www.chambres-hotes.com

The village of Tartarin is a network of narrow lanes with tall houses that offer relief from the sun's fierce heat. The lime-green shutters on the ochre façades overlook flowers growing in a Provençal courtyard. It is in this cluster of houses, inherited from the old Jewish quarter, that you'll find five guest rooms accessible via a stairway in 1930s imitation marble. Yellow ochre patinas for one, blue-and-white-striped rustic patterns for another, a low view over tiled roofs for a third. In another part of the main building, a slate-hued room, lit by a lamp with a branch as its base, adjoins another room done in turquoise and salmon. Linen sheets, battered old floor tiles, a stone trough beside an ancestral fireplace surrounded by baskets—it all helps to give this noble abode back its Provençal roots.

- Rooms: $70–$80.
- Breakfast Included.
- Closed from November 5 to December 20.

Le Mas des Arnajons

Mr. and Mrs. Viaud, 13610 Le Puy-Sainte-Réparade.
Tel: 011 33 4 42 61 86 81. Fax: 011 33 4 42 50 03 88.

Tuscany is in the air at this 18th century farmhouse splayed around a courtyard punctuated by olive trees and box trees set in earthenware pots. On beautiful days, spectacular wedding receptions have been staged here, but the most successful production is always the "Bride's Room," a scene in white on white: A frieze traced in chalk rattles off the finest love quotes literature can offer; a rice tree, with good-luck tulle bags hanging from it, is perched over an old-style bathtub covered with a bridal veil; an old barber's sink is decorated with chunks of Marseilles soap. Next door, "Pitchoune," is bedecked with raspberry hues. The other rooms vary between rural, Baroque, and Art Deco design.

- 2 rooms and 4 suites: \$80–\$150.
- Breakfast: \$13.
- Meals: \$40.
- Pool.
- Open year round.

La Haute-Terre

13100 Saint-Antonin-sur-Bayon. **Tel: 011 33 4 42 66 87 94.**
Fax: 011 33 4 42 66 87 95. www.lahauteterre.fr la.haute.terre@wanadoo.fr

This house is grounded in a valley amid the *garrigue* scrub, behind a curtain of fruit trees, the stony side of Mount St.Victoire towering above. Inside, the guest house inhabits a refined world of earthy colors, with coir floors, saffron toile de Jouy hung on a planked canopy, and Greek- or Moroccan-inspired bathrooms with plaster or *tadlakt* walls. And at breakfast time you'll find the innkeeper's daughter, Joséphine, who shows all the gifts of a great chef in the making, busy behind the stoves.

- 2 rooms: $125.
- 1 suite, sleeps 2/4: $190.
- Breakfast: $10.
- Dinner: $30.
- Pool.
- Open year round.

Vaucluse

La Maison

Michèle Rozenblat, 84340 Beaumont-du-Ventoux.
Tel: 011 33 4 90 65 15 50. Fax: 011 33 4 90 65 23 29.

It used to be a small farm surrounded by orchards, with its 18th century main house and its low walls keeping the flocks out. Down the generations, many things have been added, endowing the place with one of the prettiest courtyards in all of Provence. Tables stand beneath lime trees with a candleholder on each, from which you'll enjoy the regional specialties rich in basil and garlic. Because guests were reluctant to leave, innkeeper Michèle Rozenblat has done up three rooms with whitewashed beams. One, decked in pink with ochre-polished plastered walls and a white, quilted bedspread, is filled with Provençal furniture matched with small pieces unearthed in local shops. Another, jasmine-hued, has been turned into a suite. At the windows hang pretty red Provençal fabrics. The last, in powder blue, holds rustic furniture and still boasts grandma's antique cane chairs.

- 3 rooms: $55–$75.
- Breakfast: $10.
- Meals: $30.
- Closed from November to March.

La Grange de Jusalem

Vaucluse

Maryvonne du Lac, route de Malemort, 84380 Mazan.
Tel: 011 33 4 90 69 83 48. Fax: 011 33 4 90 69 63 53.

Maryvonne du Lac has marked this beautiful family farmhouse by roses. In zinc pots, bunches tied with ivy are set on tables covered with immaculate tablecloths from l'Orangerie. Garlands of golden roses crown the fireplace, around which fantastic meals are offered by reservation only. And since the dining experience here is the highlight of any visit, you can prolong your stay in one of the four rustic rooms. The decor runs from red hexagonal floor tiles, checkered fabrics, and Provençal patterns to lace-hemmed sheets and monogrammed pillows. On the patio, breakfast tables are set up under the arbor, where you can gaze across at Mont Ventoux, surveying the Carpentras lowlands.

- 4 rooms: $65.
- Breakfast: $7.
- Meals: $25.
- Pool.
- Open year round.

Vaucluse

La Bastide de Marie

Route de Bonnieux, Quartier de la Verrerie, 84560 Ménerbes. **Tel: 011 33 4 90 72 30 20.**
Fax: 011 33 4 90 72 54 20. www.labastidedemarie.com bastidemarie@c-h-m.com

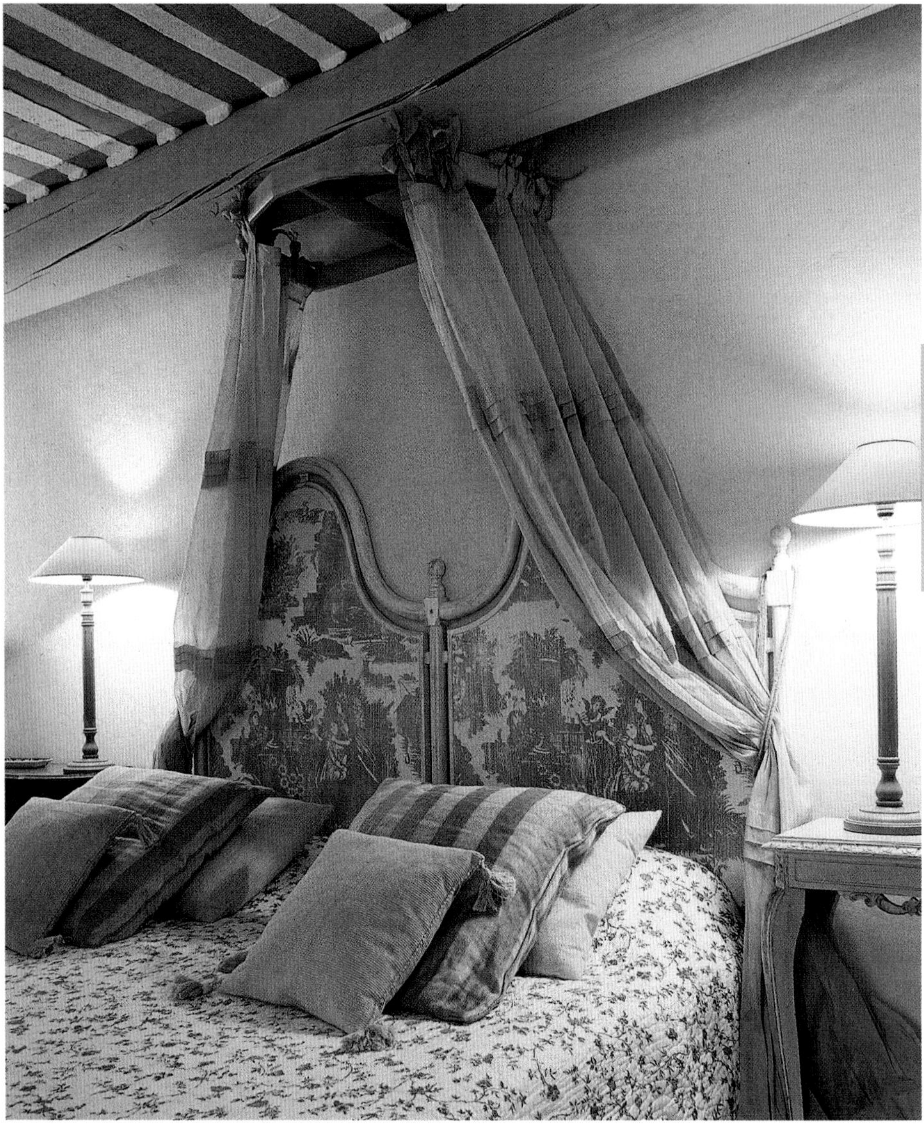

The Sibuets, well-known for their prestigious hotels in Megève, decided to establish their dream of Provençal hospitality with this small hotel. With eight rooms and six suites, La Bastide takes advantage of its Ménerbes setting, drinking in the light through half-open doors, enjoying the warmth of a huge fireplace which used to inhabit a castle's kitchen but is now installed in the living room. The various suites and rooms, walls studded with cicadas and painted in pine- wood colors, are subtle and warm. Outside, a pond sits by a terrace, right near an herb garden hemmed in by vines.

- 8 rooms: $380–$475.
- 6 suites: $570–$650.
- Breakfast included.
- Half-board dinner.
- Pools.

La Treille Muscate

Drôme

Le Village, 26270 Cliousclat. **Tel: 011 33 4 75 63 13 10.**
Fax: 011 33 4 75 63 10 79. latreillemuscate@wanadoo.fr

Imagine yourself on a summer's eve dining by candlelight on a terrace. On your plate, the kitchen has hesitated between Royans ravioli and something Oriental. It's just like this small hotel on the border of two regions: Dauphiné and Provence. When it's time for a rest, a choice of rooms in pick-me-up colors await you. Between white beams and sparkling coral, lavender and raspberry, toile de Jouy with gingham and linen sheets, you'll find bathrooms with subtle tobacco and caramel hues.

The most exotic has been inspired by the vast savannah of Kenya, with black and brick-colored walls and wrought iron and bamboo furniture brought back from Africa. The decor glorifies the colors of the south while respecting the country spirit of the village of potters and artisans that the inn calls home.

- 12 rooms: $60–$120.
- Breakfast: $10.
- Meals: $27. Restaurant closed on Wednesdays.
- Closed from December 15 to March 1.

Drôme

Une Autre Maison

Place de la République, 26110 Nyons. **Tel: 011 33 4 75 26 43 09.**
Fax: 011 33 4 75 26 93 69. www.uneautremaison.com uneautremaison@mail.dotcom.fr

Pascal Ruiz, a doctor from Lyons, loves to introduce travelers to the joys of olive country. At his townhouse, which is preceded by a terrace strewn with tubs of heather, Pascal has retained a fondness for the sunny decor of his native south, and has added raw linens, Moroccan ceramics, friezes of *azulejos* tiles, and alcoves in Cycladic blue, almond green, and ruby red. Opening onto a garden filled with ponds and different levels, the kitchen, with walls in a superb umber finish, is organized around a refectory table. And in the morning, waiting on the counter, are warm tarts and exquisite breakfast madeleines.

- 5 rooms: $100–$140.
- 1 suite: $160.
- Breakfast: $15.
- Menus: $40.
- Half-board: $110.
- Closed from November 4 to December 15.
- No dogs allowed.

La Maison Forte de Clérivaux

Drôme

Anne and Pierre Josquin, 26750 Châtillon-Saint-Jean.
Tel: 011 33 4 75 45 32 53. Fax: 011 33 4 75 71 45 43. pierre.josquin@kyxar.fr

This fortified house has watched century follow century in a hamlet overlooking the patchwork of a cultivated valley. You have to hear Anne and Pierre Josquin talk passionately about the Middle Ages in general, and about their residence in particular, and their determination to save the ancestral craft techniques, down to the smallest detail. Large bay windows flood the house with light, but everything dating from the 16th and 17th centuries has been preserved. The wooden ceilings, taken down, dismantled, treated, and reinstalled, now gaze down upon a contemporary staircase which fits perfectly with the decor. Bedrooms are clad in putty-colored linen and filled with beautifully made furniture in the rustic and Belle Epoque styles. In one of the bathrooms, like a wink at history, a small harquebus window has been kept in the corner of a tub. On nice days, breakfast is served in the garden on the low-walled terrace.

- 4 rooms: $60.
- Breakfast included.
- Closed from January 10 to February 10.
- No dogs allowed.

La Maison de Soize

Nicole and Jean-François Convercy, place de l'Eglise, 26230 Colonzelle.
Tel/fax: 011 33 4 75 46 58 58.

"Violette," "Iris," "Eglantine" ("Dogrose"), "Pâquerette" ("Daisy"), and "Capucine" ("Nasturtium")... the bedrooms line the colors up. Set within the tall stone walls of a small village in the Provençal region of the Drôme, La Maison de Soize has a southerly feel to it and the jovial mood that goes with it. Taking its name from the innkeepers' young daughter, "Violette" has an exquisite spring flower ambience and comes with a small country shower room. "Capucine" has a palette of lemon-yellow and bitter orange, accompanied by a bright yellow bathroom with madras touches. "Pâquerette," in chick yellow and delicate lime green, houses an adorable child's wardrobe. "Eglantine" offers a duet in perfect harmony: Art Nouveau/Art Deco. As for "Iris," in blazing purple, it announces summer's return under a yellow, topstitched canopy. An amazing swimming pool, suspended over a stone arch, is open in the summer.

- 5 rooms: $70–$80.
- Breakfast included.
- Meals: $25.
- Pool.
- Closed from November 1 to Easter.

Le Clair de Plume

Drôme

Mr. Valadeau, place du Mail, 26230 Grignan. **Tel: 011 33 4 75 91 81 30. Fax: 011 33 4 75 91 81 31.**
www.chateauxhotelsfrance.com/clairplume clairplume@chateauxhotels.com

All-night parties, movies filmed on location, star-sightings... the village of Grignan has become a must in Provence. And Le Clair de Plume distills all of the village's moods. The hotel is at once contemporary and old-fashioned, offering up Moroccan bamboo benches, still-lifes painted with gold leaf, bedspreads the color of sage or citrus, Berber plaids, upholstered chairs, and wicker chests. The typically Provençal vaulted kitchen speaks to a time when this pink-fronted mansion was a monastery. These days, it is a hotel featured in the Châteaux et Hôtels de France, a place where you will instantly savor the promise of breakfast in the garden beneath an arbor of vines and the warmth of a July evening in the mingling scents of rose and honeysuckle.

- 10 rooms: $90–$170.
- Breakfast included.
- Open year round.

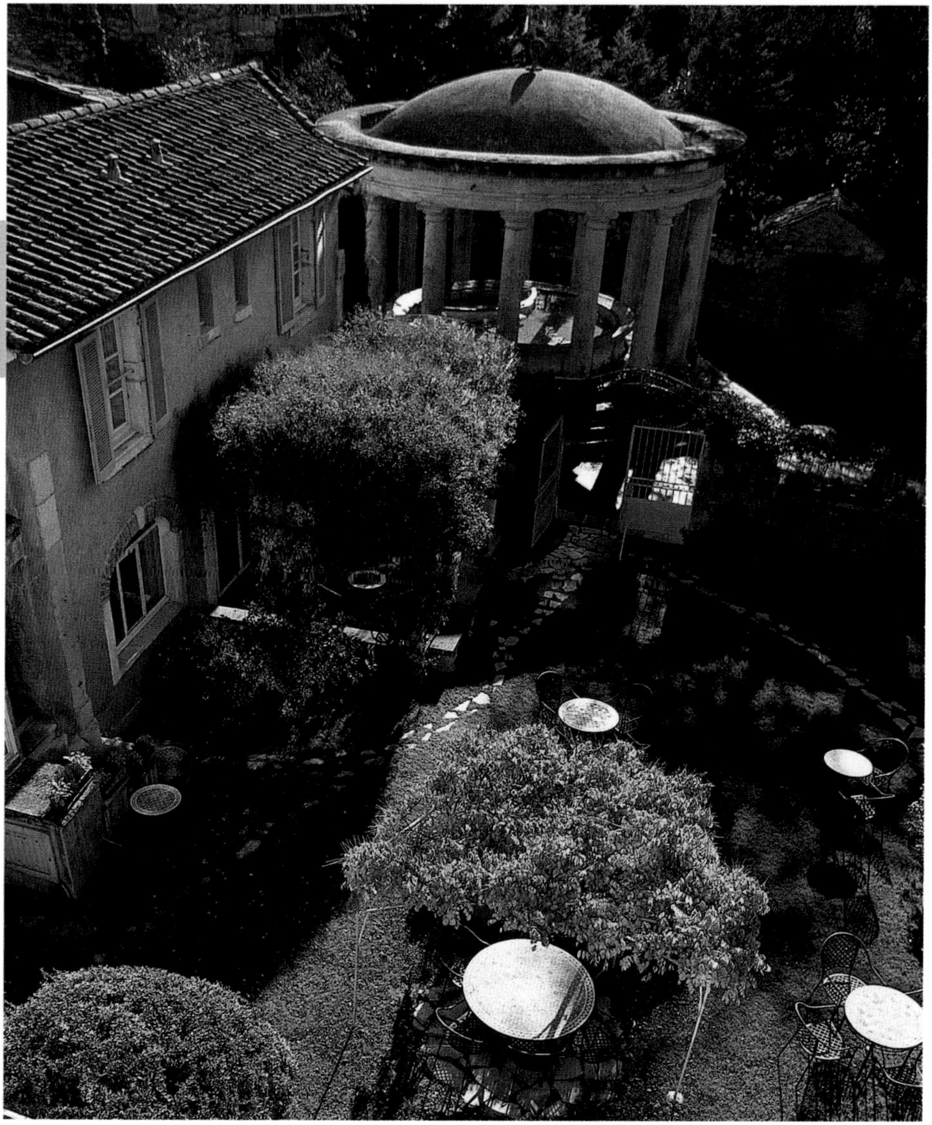

La Santoline

07460 Beaulieu. **Tel: 011 33 4 75 39 01 91. Fax: 011 33 4 75 39 38 79.**
www.lasantoline.com contacts@lasantoline.com

Near the Ardèche gorge, a stone's throw from the astonishing Païolive Wood filled with white oak and petrified rocks, this small hotel boasts the secrets of true hospitality beneath its 16th century vaults, its embossed stairs, and its stone nooks. Seven carefully decorated rooms combine country furniture, linen curtains cut from ancient embroidered sheets, topstitched and quilted bedspreads, and maritime color schemes with the summery pastels of lime and sunflower. The garden furniture around the swimming pool is especially elegant. It all serves to help summer live on in the aromas of the surrounding *garrigue*.

- 7 rooms: $60–$110.
- 1 suite: $110.
- Breakfast: $10.
- Dinner: $30.
- Pool.
- Closed from October to May.

Le Couradou

Ardèche

Annie and Xavier Destrade, 07150 Labastide-de-Virac.
Tel: 011 33 4 75 38 64 75. Fax: 011 33 4 75 38 68 26.

You'll gaze at the mauve glow of the sun setting over the Cévennes from the terrace of this stone building. Le Couradou is filled with nooks and crannies, stairs, vaults and different levels, mixing styles and colors in a shrewdly orchestrated Bohemian harmony. If the "Blanche" ("White") room has a very definite Art Deco note to it, the "Rose" ("Pink") room lies drowsily amid pale flowers and lavender hues. The "Verte" ("Green") room displays a maiden's romanticism in a riot of crimson peonies, while the "Jaune" ("Yellow") room brings a bit of the countryside indoors. There's yellow and fuchsia again for the "Indian" room. The "Marocaine" ("Moroccan") room organizes its Scheherazade-inspired decoration around a genuine camel-driver's chest. Throughout, flashes of wit abound, such as the bathroom linen presented in hanging baskets, and the Oriental ironwork holding down a canopy of blueish drapes.

- 6 rooms: $80–$130.
- Breakfast included.
- Meals: $45.
- Pool.
- Closed in December and January.

Le Vivier

04400 Enchastrayes.
Tel: 011 33 4 92 81 19 65. Fax: 011 33 4 92 81 27 21.

An oil lamp gives off its coppery glow beneath an ancient sheepfold haunted by nooks and crannies. Logs crackle in the hearth. Leather armchairs invite you into them. The billiard table waits until supper's over to gather the guests at this residence set up at the end of a forest tract. With owners Joël and Nicole Cézanne, the term "being welcomed as if you were with friends" assumes its fullest meaning. The bedrooms are in the same spirit, expressing their warm tones between larch planks and Provençal cottons. And from your bed you'll be under the wing of the Chapeau de Gendarme—the Cop's Hat—one of the most striking peaks in the Ubaye valley. Sweet dreams.

- 4 rooms: $55.
- Additional bed: $17.
- Breakfast included.
- Meals (reservation required): $30.
- Half-board: $45.
- Closed 10 days in June, and one month between October and November.

La Crémerie du Glacier

333, route des Rives, Les Bossons, 74400 Chamonix.
Tel/fax: 011 33 4 50 55 90 10.

You might think this was a stage setting in a light opera, given a boost with pastel yellow and blue. In a Beatrix Potter meets "Heidi in the Land of Mont Blanc"-like setting, Danièle and Chacha welcome winter guests to their alpine abode. It can be said, though, that with its soft-yellow façade, its blue shutters, and its many-colored garlands, the house doesn't fit the local mold. Actually, it's an old dairy where people used to come to sample local specialties. Danièle still offers these in her little bistro, in a fairy-tale decor echoed in the bedrooms filled with patchwork quilts and colored paneling. You can even rent a small wooden cottage, known as a *mazot*. Chacha brought several of these down from Alpine pastures, done them up, and planted them in the nearby meadows. Like mini-suites or dollhouses, the cottages are filled with painted furniture and pine wreaths, and are sure to delight the young at heart.

- 7 rooms: $40–$50 half-board per person.
- Closed from September 30 to December 15.

Les Servages

Armelle and Patrick Linglin, 74300 Araches Les Carroz. **Tel: 011 33 4 50 90 01 62.**
Fax: 011 33 4 50 90 39 41. www.carroz.com/servages servages@carroz.com

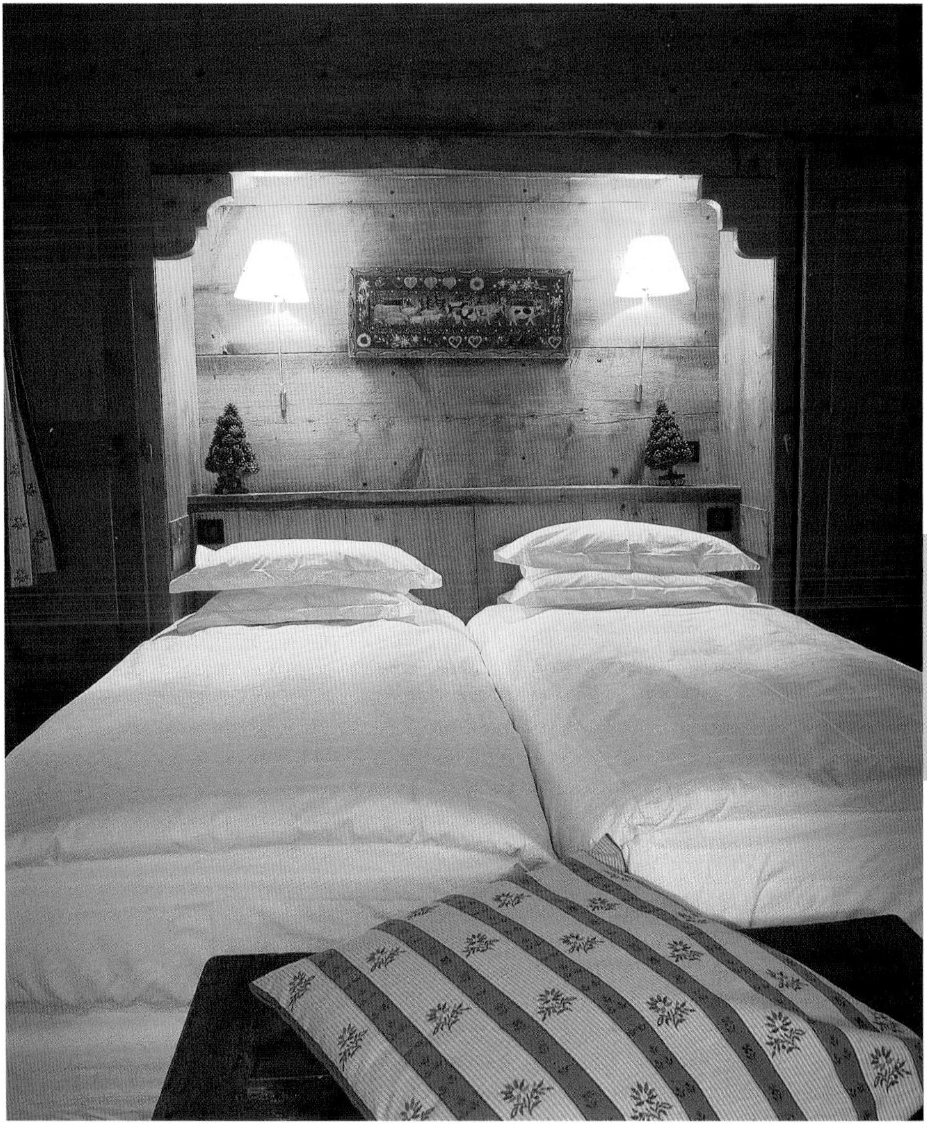

Roofs made in the Swiss style using thin, rounded wooden slats, pale wood with heart cut-outs on the balconies... It is here at Les Servages that Armelle Linglin, a former ski champion, and her husband Patrick have realized their dream. By recycling everything that was recyclable on this old mountain farm, they turned it into a warm chalet. Friends came, and then friends of friends. Today they welcome guests to snuggle in front of the fire in a club chair and enjoy the Savoyard aromas wafting from the kitchen. Travelers take refuge in the cozy cocoon of rooms filled with fabrics flecked with edelweiss, with magnificent adjoining bathrooms in charcoal-gray granite, and in surprising alcoves with black and white shapes cut out in the felt fabric of the curtains. Selected fabrics, teddy bear-brown fleece comforters and matching teddy bears—everything here has been designed to reconcile skiing with the art of living well.

- 4 rooms: $160–$180.
- 1 suite: $220.
- Breakfast: $15.
- Half-board: $120–$145.
- Open year round.

L'Hôtel des Cîmes

Le Chinaillon, 74450 Le Grand-Bornand. **Tel: 011 33 4 50 27 00 38.**
Fax: 011 33 4 50 27 08 46. www.hotel-les-cimes.com hotel-les-cimes@hct.net

At the end of a valley studded with stout chalets and bulb-shaped belfries, this small mountain hotel designed by the owner is as pretty as a picture. She loves all things heart-shaped, and has scattered hearts here, there, and everywhere in the ten small rooms, embroidered on linen sheets, cut out in fleece-lined quilted bedspreads, woven onto colorful patchwork quilts. Her house smells of cereals and spices, beeswax and tea-time *rissoles*. She's enlisted an artist from Annecy to create a symphony of soft colors which is harmonious with her heart theme, inspired by the green of mountain pastures, the blue of glaciers, and the pink of rhododendrons. Bright tiles, white comforters, and chunky pillows form a warm world which would still be welcome by its mountain-farmer forebears, whose portraits are hung around the hotel.

- 10 rooms: $90– $150.
- Breakfast included.
- Closed from April 28 to June 14, and from September 15 to November 23.

Le Chalet-hôtel de la Croix-Fry

Marie-Ange and Isabelle Guelpa-Veyrat, route du Col, 74230 Manigod.
Tel: 011 33 4 50 44 90 16. Fax: 011 33 4 50 44 94 87. www.hotelchaletcroixfry.com

With its wooden shell plunged beneath a hood of snow, this chalet hotel has everything you could want in a mountain setting. The fireplace warms the coldest of alpine evenings, and you can watch the snow fall from one of the rustic window seats covered with plump cushions. Everywhere, teddy bears perch on the arms of chairs, surrounded by Savoy pottery and old furniture hunted down by owner Marie-Ange Guelpa-Veyrat and her daughter Isabelle. They are the heiresses of a line of mountain folk whose calling has been followed ever since Grandma Karavi bought this mountain farm in 1939 and turned it into a delightful inn. The table is heavy with family specialties as well as inventive new dishes adapted to seasonal produce. And come evening, guests wander off to the ten rooms underneath pale wooden beams upstairs... and dream of another snowy white morning.

- 5 rooms: starting at $120.
- 5 suites: starting at $170.
- Brunch: $20.
- Menus: $25–$70.
- Closed from April 15 to June 15, September 15 to December 15.

Hôtel Saint-Martin

73440 Saint-Martin-de-Belleville. **Tel: 011 33 4 79 00 88 00. Fax: 011 33 4 79 00 88 39.**
www.hotel-stmartin.com hotelsaintmartin@wanadoo.fr

On the edge of the world's largest skiable estate, the Hôtel Saint-Martin espouses the style of its immaculately preserved village with stone-slabbed roofs, stone walls, hanging balconies, and larch wood shingling. The great living room, with its deep armchairs and old-time photographs , inspire conversation around the crackling fire. Wood is everywhere, creating a warm ambience which you also find in the bedrooms, with their white comforters trimmed in fabric, the rust and slate-gray pointillés, and the ivory drapes set off by plaid blankets. With views over the ski runs, the village, and its hamlets, each room has its own personality. Up in the "loft" you'll enjoy Savoy specialties in a more relaxed atmosphere; for more conventional, less rustic cuisine, head to the hotel dining room.

- 27 rooms: $90–$200 half-board.
- 5 apartments: $995–$3,300 for a week.
- Sauna, fitness center, steam room.
- Closed from April 15 to December 15.

Gard

Le Château de Saint-Maximin

Jean-Marc Perry, rue du Château, 30700 Saint-Maximin.
Tel: 011 33 4 66 03 44 16. Fax: 011 33 4 66 03 42 98. info@chatostmaximin.com

Behind its fortified mass, the castle offers the tranquility of a resort and the moodiness of a village castle. Its hanging gardens, replanted with olives, overlook a swimming pool lined with green mosaics.

- 2 rooms and 3 suites: $100–$275.
- Breakfast included.
- Dinner (reservation required) from Wednesday to Sunday: $40–$45.
- Closed in February.

Racine lived here, dispatched to his paternal uncle to be put on the straight and narrow. The new owner has set out to demystify the place without denying its origins. Jean-Marc Perry has filled the rooms with an Art Deco ambience, combining ivory, caramel, and tobacco. Fabrics, silks, rugs, and accessories by Théophile, Pinto, and Casa Lopez, and 1940s furniture make up the decor. The rooms are named after Racine's heroines. "Bérénice," the most feminine of them, is done in silk madras with floral linings featuring bunches of faded roses. The room opens out beneath an arbor where, from sunrise on, gourmet breakfasts are served. The rooms have no television or telephones, which certainly helps maintain the castle's serenity.

Le Mas de l'Amandier

Gard

Camp Galhan, 30720 Ribaute-les-Tavernes. **Tel: 011 33 4 66 83 87 06.**
Fax: 011 33 4 66 83 87 69. mas.amandier@free.fr

He was a photographer, she, a fashion designer. No doubt about it, owners Dominique Bernard and Sophie Lasbleiz were made for each other. Nurtured on the same love of beauty, natural materials, and forms, they chose to moor their dreams at the gateway to the Cévennes. This ancient 12th century mansion in a small rustic hamlet was pining after years of neglect. While retaining its history, Dominique and Sophie have breathed life back into the property with wrought iron beds, shepherds' beds in an almond-green velvety finish, mosquito netting as light as a gust of wind, and bedspreads scattered with poppies and violets. And then there are the bathrooms, all done in meerschaum and turquoise. And by using Salernes tiles in pastel shades mixed with terra-cotta, Dominique has designed floors that give added depth to the room they inhabit.

- 3 rooms: $60–$120.
- Suites: $80–$120.
- Breakfast included.
- Meals (reservation required): $25.
- Open year round.

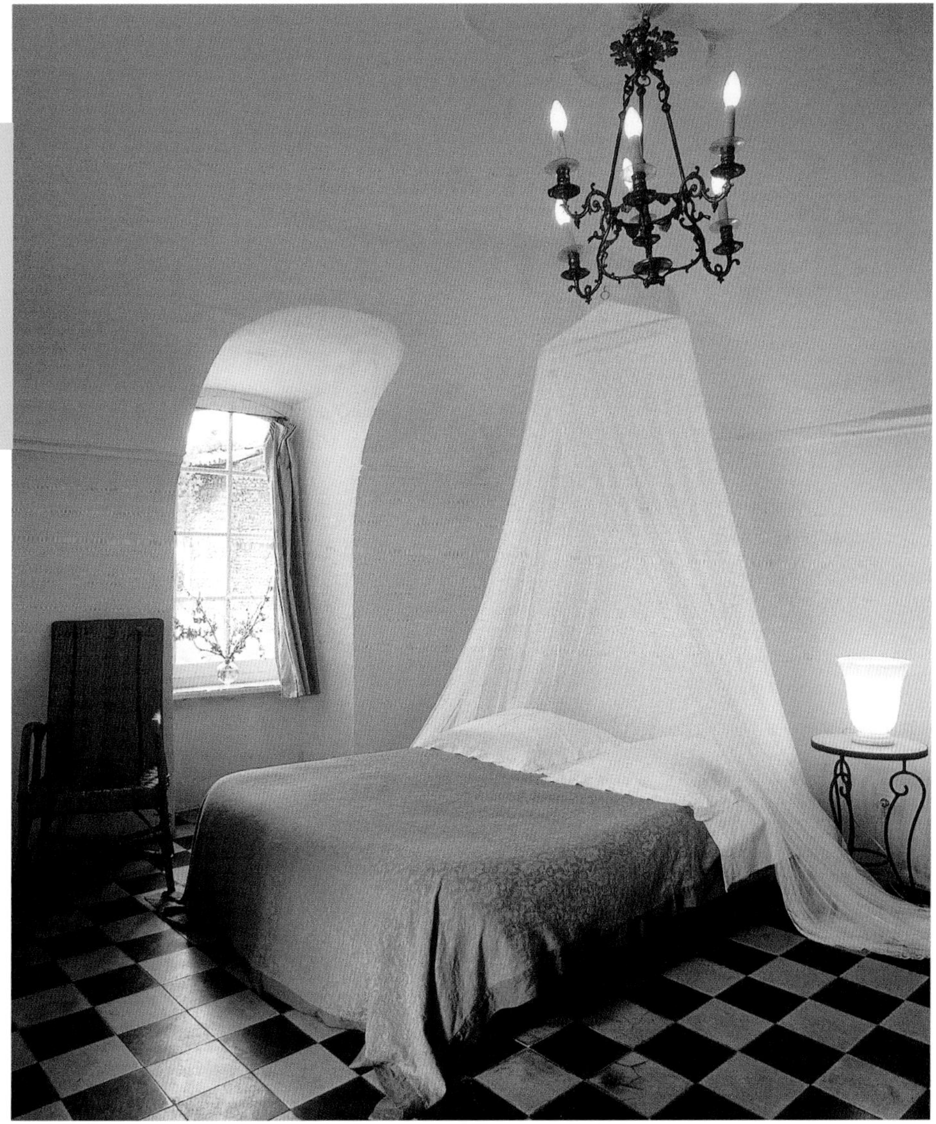

Le Mas Bazan

Annie and Paul Favier, domaine du Mas Bazan, 66200 Alénya. **Tel: 011 33 4 68 22 98 26.**
Fax: 011 33 4 68 22 97 37. http://perso.wanadoo.fr/mas.bazan mas.bazan@wanadoo.fr

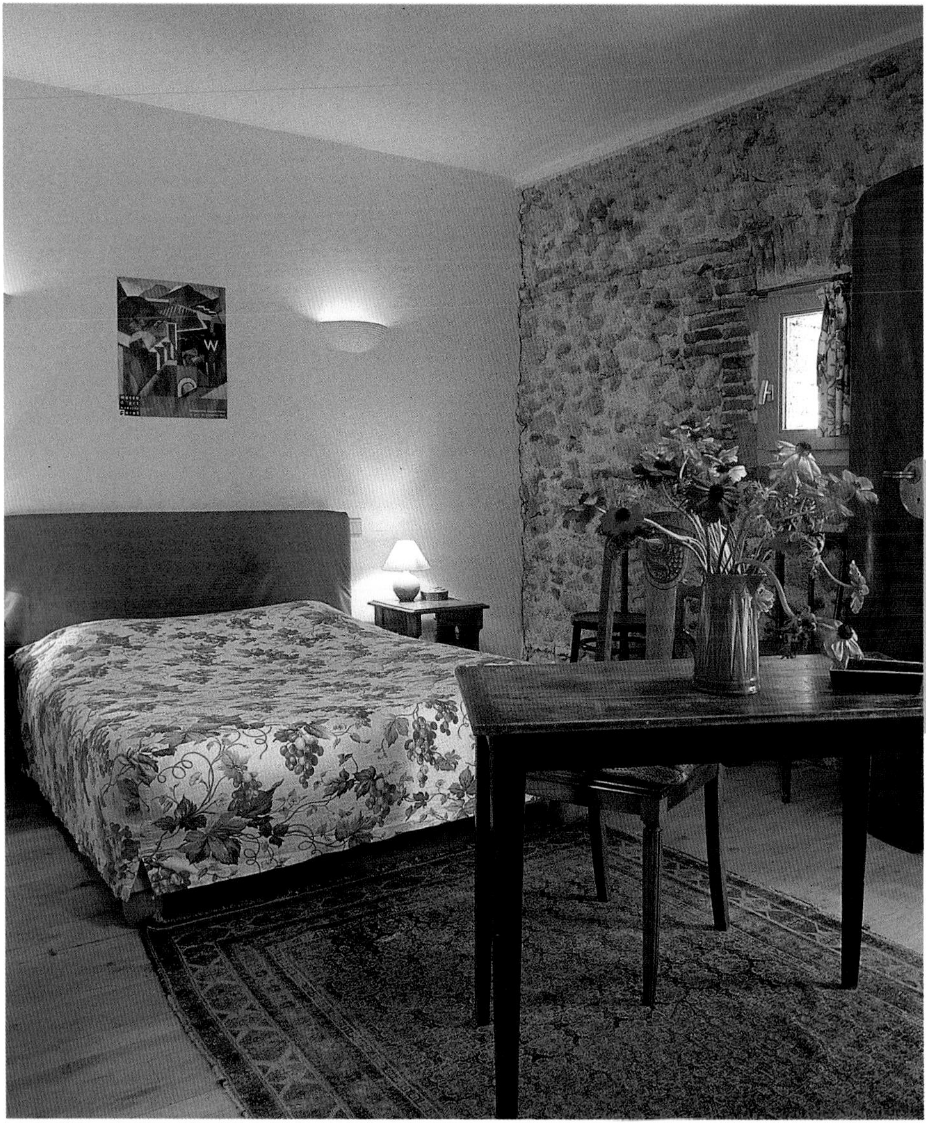

Set just back from the beaches is a winegrowing property in the heart of the Roussillon orchards. Around the pool you sample Rivesaltes muscat and talk about your day. This is how it is at Le Mas Bazan, in the warmth of summer evenings. With their genuine sense of welcome and hospitality, Annie and Paul Favier have supplied their inn with the warm atmosphere of a real friend's house. Roses climb up brick walls, a lounge has been installed inside former stables with their hayracks still inside. The Art Deco furniture is enhanced by touches of wit placed here and there by one or two artist friends. And upstairs, in the four rooms that occupy the old attic, you'll stumble onto a nostalgic collection of country furniture, warmed by floral fabrics, printed with bunches of grapes, and eiderdowns made of Catalan cotton.

- 4 rooms and 1 suite: $45–$60.
- Breakfast included.
- Meals: $25.
- Pool.
- Closed from December 15 to January 15.

Laurence Jonquères d'Oriola

9, rue des Cavaliers, 66200 Corneilla-del-Vercol.
Tel: 011 33 4 68 22 12 67. Cell: 011 33 6 13 37 49 74.

This family property, an 18th century mansion with unostentatious decor but an atmosphere of elegance, is worth a night's stay. Beautiful hexagonal brick-red tiles on the floors, furniture scouted down in flea markets, and a pool table all lend it a certain playful soul. The rooms are named after famous horses, so you will have a choice between the "Olympic" bedroom, Iberian in inspiration and dedicated to Lutteur, winner of the Tokyo Olympic games; or the one named in honor of Pomone, world champion in Buenos Aires, livened up by its white cottons. There is also "Voulette," a room that plays with shades of gray and yellow, named after a mischievous little mare, winner of many a Grand Prix, who could blithely jump six feet high. In the garden, hidden behind beautiful ironwork and veiled by a cascade of bougainvillea, is a small apartment with pine furniture. Nothing showy, but a delightful dwelling in a setting where people with horses, or people who are fond of them, will surely feel welcome.

- 3 rooms: $55.
- 1 suite, sleeps 4: $95.
- Breakfast included.
- Open year round.

La Vieille Demeure

Christine and Jean-Louis Vignaud. 4, rue de Llobet. 66440 Torreilles.
Tel/fax: 011 33 4 68 28 45 71. www.la-vieille-demeure.com vignaud.christine@wanadoo.fr

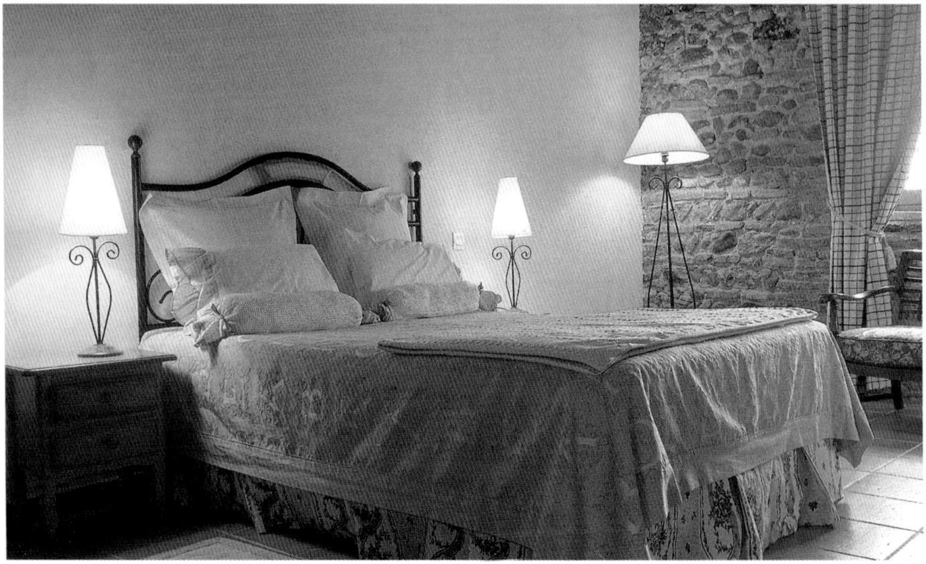

It's grapefruit, mandarin, and lemon tones for the bedrooms in this former 17th century baronial house in Toreilles, a sunny Pyrenean village. Its new owners have managed to restore it, keeping its traditional spirit intact while imbuing it with the mood of the moment. The interiors are yellow and red ochre. Bare beams look down on terra-cotta floors, high brick steps, and hand-painted walls. A peaceful patio visited by birds is a nice breakfast spot, and a good place to take in the views of orange trees and the summertime citrus garden that thrives in this Catalan climate.

■ 4 rooms and 2 suites: $80–$150.
■ Breakfast included.
■ Closed in January and February.

La Villa Duflot

André Duflot, rond-point Albert-Donnezan, 66000 Perpignan. **Tel: 011 33 4 68 56 67 67.**
Fax: 011 33 4 68 56 54 05. www.villa-duflot.com contact@villa-duflot.com

An intimate hotel set in a business district is quite a daring move. Eleven years ago, André Duflot made this crazy wager. Today the Villa has become one of the leading addresses for Perpignan and for performers on tour. For the tenth anniversary of the property, André Duflot installed a new wine center offering the best vintages of the Languedoc. And you can sample them beneath the cypress-green parasols on the terrace, or in the shade of the patio, or out by the pool, or in the privacy of your room. Speaking of the rooms, they're done with contemporary comfort in mind, sporting sofas and comfy armchairs. In the polished-marble bathrooms, the sense of space has been enhanced by mirrors. The restaurant, serving Catalan cuisine, perpetuates the elegant atmosphere found throughout the Villa.

- 24 rooms: $100-$200.
- Suites: $110–$250.
- Breakfast: $10.
- Meals: $32–$40.
- Pool.
- Open year round.

Le Grand Guilhem

Mr. and Mrs. Contrepois, chemin du Col de la Serre, 11360 Cascastel.
Tel: 011 33 4 68 45 86 67. Fax: 011 33 4 68 45 29 58. gguilhem@aol.com

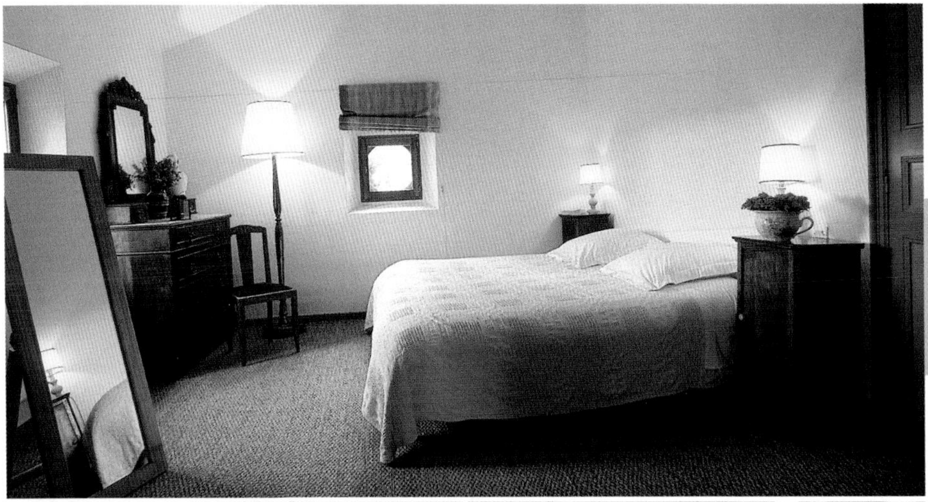

A few years ago, when they were looking to settle in vineyard country, Gilles and Séverine Contrepois purchased this handsome winegrower's house, a typical Corbières *maison de maître* mansion. It had hardly been lived in since it was built in 1870 so there was nothing artificial about it. Revamped, and rejuvenated with contemporary colors, its walls now boasts garlands of printed roses which lead to the upstairs rooms—all named after a Languedoc grape variety: "Carignan," with gold and fuchsia hues brightened up by turquoise, cobalt, and emerald prints, and accompanied by a Cycladic blue bathroom. Vanilla shades for "Syrah." Mauve, dark purple, and wine-lees stripes for "Muscat." And this symphony of colors is followed up by a real, musical one, when Gilles, winner of the first prize for saxophone at the Narbonne Conservatory, combines his two passions, music and wine, at weekends of wine tasting, music, and fine food.

- 4 rooms: $60–$75.
- Breakfast included.
- Pool.
- Open year round.

Le Domaine du Haut-Gléon

Aude

Villesèque-des-Corbières, 11360 Durban. **Tel: 011 33 4 68 48 85 95.**
Fax: 011 33 4 68 48 46 20. contact@hautgleon.com www.hautgleon.com

The delicate blue shutters of the outbuildings open on to a carefully tended property, ringed by hills, covered with vines planted with the blessing of Gléon, a 7th century saint who still has his chapel here. This elegant winegrowing estate accommodates, within its former shepherd's and grape-picker's houses, guest rooms inspired by the works of artists in residence. Every year their works are supported by a patronage geared to contemporary art. So the room "Alicante" is theatrically set between tall whitewashed walls, with a narrow stairway climbing up to its spare bathroom installed in the mezzanine. The next room has a sheep-fold atmosphere. More toned-down shades beneath slate-gray walls for a third room. The others are like a great bouquet of vibrant colors: raspberry, cloudy skies, blue, and grass-green around sophisticated country furniture.

- 6 rooms: $70.
- Breakfast included.
- Open year round.

Aude

La Mignoterie

Mr. and Mrs. Mignot, 11220 Fajac-en-Val.
Tel/fax: 011 33 4 68 79 71 42. mignoterie@wanadoo.fr

Barely ten miles from Carcassonne, this nice couple of city-dwellers on the verge of settling down to a well-worked-out early retirement operate this storied residence. Local rumor has it that in the early 1960s, Charles Trénet wrote some of his hits here. And as every legend is nurtured by a grain of truth, the "Trénet" world is re-created with the fireplace with its Minotaur's legs. You may even glimpse a few mischievous elves running along the landings and the bleached parquet floors. The four rooms combine austerity and a touch of madness. They exude easy comfort with their shades of pink, purple, mauve, plum, and white, with recycled furniture, a portrait of the Medicis, a touch of Baroque, and a hint of Surrealism completing the curious passage. No doubt, La Mignoterie will seduce those looking to venture off the beaten track.

- 4 rooms: $50–$55.
- Breakfast included.
- Meals: $20.
- Closed in January and February.

La Méjanassère

Aveyron

Véronique and Frédéric Forveille, 12140 Entraygues.
Tel/fax: 011 33 5 65 44 54 76.

This farmhouse inn has taken over an old hamlet filled with stone-slab roofs and stone walls covered with old roses, foot bridges, vaults, and mossy steps. It is a farm sitting on an ancient Roman site where the sarcophagi have by turns been transformed into troughs for livestock and then fountains for people. Inside, hues of turquoise, celadon green, and salmon pink now coat the old hay loft and the cow shed. In the restaurant, you'll find an earthy ambience, where the beams support a ceiling painted Flanders blue. Here, innkeeper Véronique Forveille mixes flowers and wild herbs for an authentic country fare which is both natural and tasty.

- 2 rooms: $40.
- 1 cottage, sleeps 3
- Breakfast included.
- Meals: $20.

Aveyron

La Ferme de Moulhac

Claudine Long, 12210 Laguiole. **Tel/fax: 011 33 5 65 44 33 25.**
Cell: 011 33 6 07 30 55 77. http://perso.wanadoo.fr/moulhac

When Claudine Long and her husband decided to open four guest rooms in the former cow shed of their livestock farm, they deliberately opted for an avant-garde and slightly off-kilter style. Behind a glass door, you enter a railway sleeper staked out with pebbles. In the breakfast room you also find this half-Art Brut and half-contemporary-art decor around the fireplace, where a face-shaped stone, acting as a counterweight, gazes at you while you recline into an old leather armchair or sit on a wrought iron chair. Upstairs, there is the same combination of raw materials—objects of the past put to a different use and design—such as a length of chestnut wood cut diagonally which acts as the headboard in one of the rooms. And to breathe some life and character into a door made of copper, tinted with acid and wax, the Longs thought nothing of dragging it along the road and covering it with gravel before driving over it.

- 4 rooms: $40–$50.
- Breakfast included.
- Pets: $5.
- Open year round.

L'Hôtel du Vieux-Pont

Aveyron

Nicole and Michèle Fagegaltier, 12390 Belcastel. **Tel: 011 33 5 65 64 52 29.**
Fax: 011 33 5 65 64 44 32. www.hotelbelcastel.com

With its old humpback bridge and church complete with recumbent Romanesque figures, Belcastel is a village from another era. You can have a chat with an angler shrouded in morning mists, or you can have your breakfast with your bare feet resting in the grass. So as not to interrupt the mood, the bedrooms in the Hôtel du Vieux-Pont are not cluttered with useless things. They will seduce you with their sincere atmosphere, with a burst of raspberry on a stylish armchair, a sculpture of branches against a spotless wall, and fern-like tones against ivory fabric. And when you have admired all this, you will treat yourself to the restaurant, with its gourmet dishes prepared by chef Nicole Fagegaltier, whose renown has spread well beyond the borders of the region.

- 7 rooms: $70–$85.
- Half-board: starting at $80.
- Additional bed: $12.
- Breakfast: $12.
- Menus: $25–$65.
- Open year round.

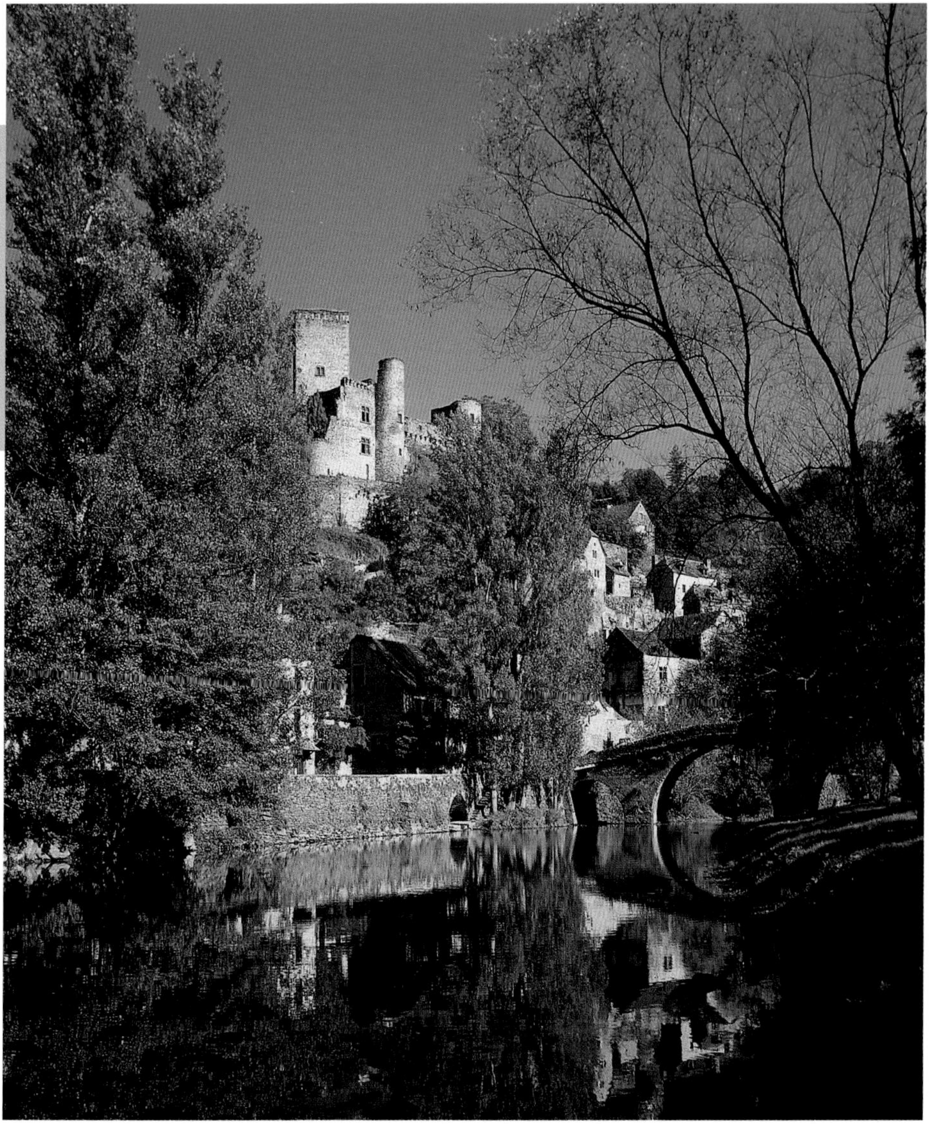

La Musardière

34, avenue de la République, 12100 Millau. **Tel: 011 33 5 65 60 20 63.**
Fax: 011 33 5 65 59 78 13. hotel-lamusardiere@wanadoo.fr

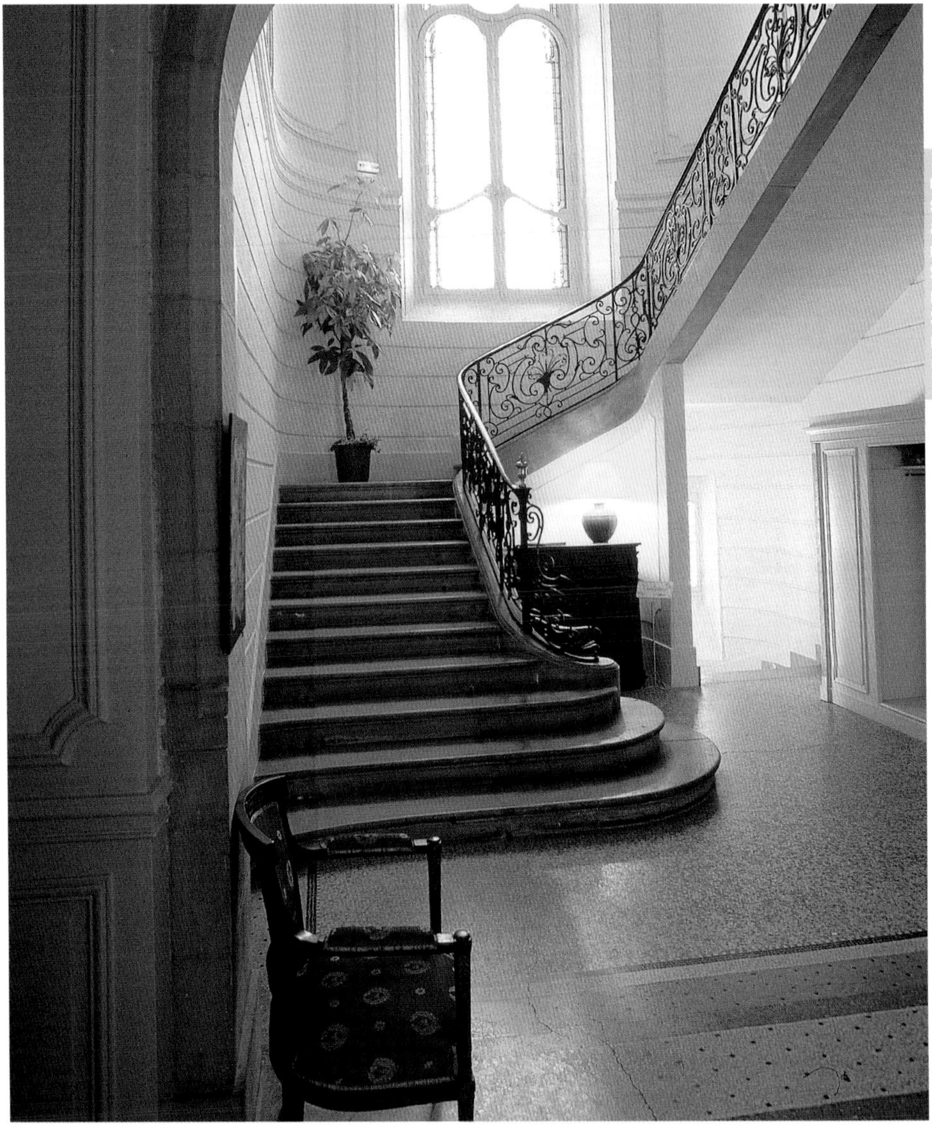

Built in 1860 by a wealthy family of glove-makers, La Musardière was renovated a few seasons ago and turned into a hotel, offering elegant rooms beneath high, molded ceilings. A monumental skylight brings out the ochre in the cement tiling, which leads to a stairway with a magnificent wrought iron banister. Rooms and suites alike have the look and feel of apartments, with two or three steps leading from one level to another, stained-glass windows, and woodwork. A few favorites are "Passion," filled with red roses; "Manon," with its honey and ivory tones; "Violette," done in mauve. The most current, though, is the "Chambre des amoureux" or "Lover's Room," completely unadorned, with, as a centerpiece, a spotlessly white bed, the effect offset by a multi-colored floral chandelier.

- 14 rooms and suites: starting at $65.
- Breakfast: $12.
- Menus: $18–$50.
- Open year round.

La Villa Calvi

Haute-Corse

Mr. Pinelli, Chemin de Notre-Dame de la Serra, 20260 Calvi. **Tel: 011 33 4 95 65 10 10.**
Fax: 011 33 4 95 65 10 50. www.hotel-lavilla.com jean-pierre.pinelli@wanadoo.fr

With its rooms all fresh and welcoming in their shades of sunny straw and Mediterranean blue, this hotel is a home away from home. Season after season it has been enlarged without compromising either the natural beauty of its setting or the quality of its welcome. At La Villa, the commitment is to the art of living well. It is here that the influences of the Corsican soul, the hanging gardens of nearby Italy, and the French influences of cozy comfort in lounges and alcoves all come together in style throughout the 26 rooms and 23 apartments. When it's time for dinner, the lights go on opposite the huge swimming pool as the sky pales. Then the view of the Bay of Calvi, the ring of mountains toppling into the sea, and the sleepy old citadel is unforgettable.

- 26 rooms: $260–$550.
- 23 apartments: $420–$800.
- Breakfast: $25.
- Meals: $65.
- Pools, tennis.
- Closed in January and February.

La Signoria

Route de la Forêt de Bonifato, 20260 Calvi. **Tel: 011 33 4 95 65 93 00.**
Fax: 011 33 4 95 65 38 77. www.hotel-la-signoria.com info@hotel-la-signoria.com

This 17th century Genoese residence is decorated with the Italian frescoes of its origins. In the rooms of the main building, furnished with chic flea market finds and Baroque and Art Deco pieces, the atmosphere is rather rustic, more like a family home: Old paintings share the walls with large contemporary canvases. In the old stables, at garden level, damasks and taffetas unveil a new kind of privacy, reminiscent of a low-lit Japanese *ryokan.* A dark passage lined with alcoves has been washed with bright colors—azure, leaf green, terra-cotta, and fuchsia—matching the recycled cement floor tiles. A huge deck, staked out by pots of citrus trees, leads to the pool, where summer meals are served.

- 15 rooms: $125–$300.
- 3 suites: $190–$490.
- Additional bed: $25.
- Breakfast: $20.
- Half-board: starting at $65.
- Pool, tennis.
- Closed from October 31 to April 1.
- No pets allowed.

La Casa Musicale

Jérôme Casalonga, 20220 Pigna. **Tel: 011 33 4 95 61 77 31.**
jerome-casalonga@casa-musicale.org www.casa-musicale.org

Surrounded by bay laurels and bougainvilleas, La Casa Musicale opens its blue gates onto a house that seems forever young, a gathering place for musicians from Balagne as well as visitors to this little village on a mountainside. Its terrace, overlooking the sea, may be modest, but it's a haven of peace and quiet. It is here that the staff will serve up delicious local fare prepared with an understanding and appreciation of simple, pure tastes. Old tiles lead to rooms named after all things musical. Their lime-washed walls of glacier blue and straw yellow are overtaken by frescoes. Throw open the shutters for views of hills covered in a patchwork of crops and for the sea beyond. When evenings turn cooler, take refuge in the vaulted room of the old oil mill, where one or two forgotten scores, a guitar, and a trombone will always remind you of the place's calling.

- 7 rooms: $45–$85.
- Breakfast: $7.
- Meals: $25–$35.

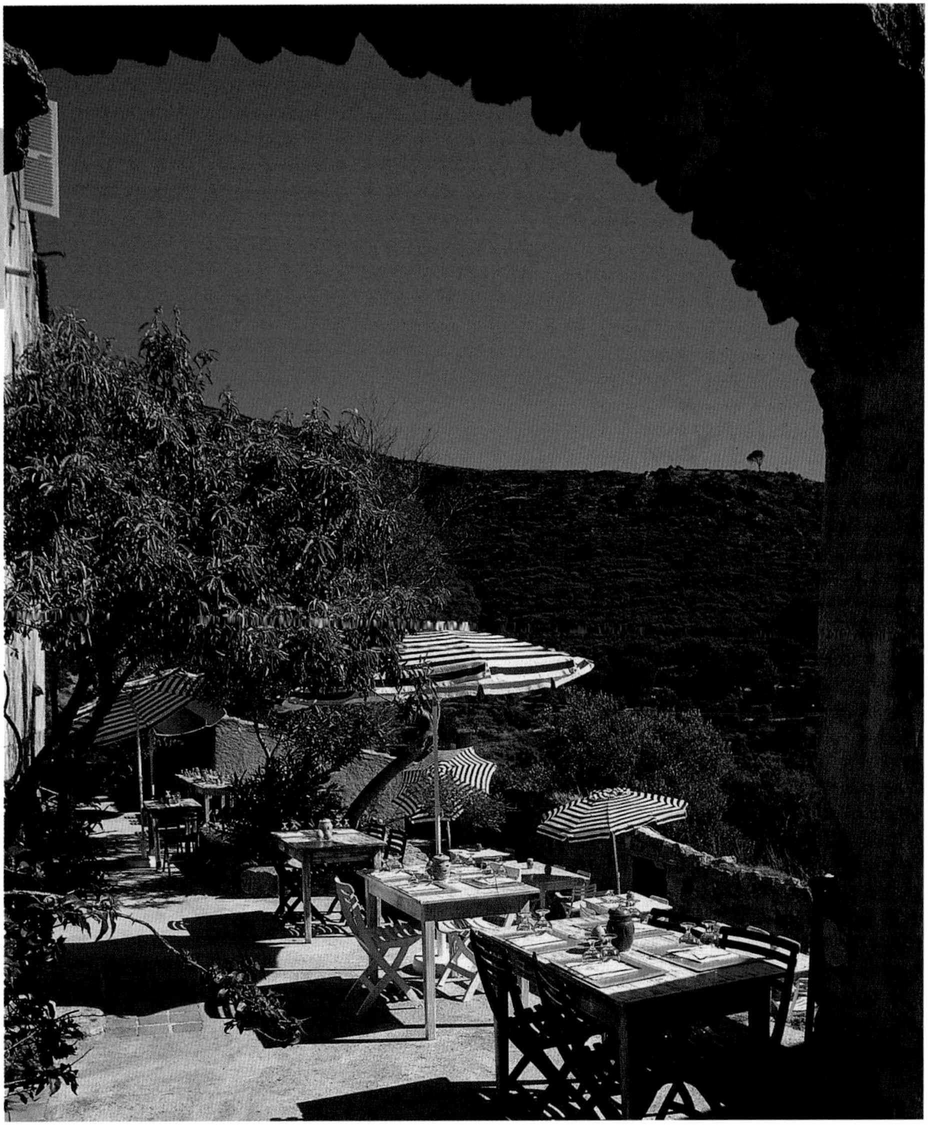

La Casa Corsa

Mr. and Mrs. Doumens, Aquanera. Prunete, 20221 Cervione.
Tel: 011 33 4 95 38 01 40.

At the gateway to La Castagnicce, where the plains stop and the mountains start as they near the sea, thrives an unexpected guest house. Manned by a diligent innkeeper who has mastered the art of removing every last speck of dust, Mr. Doumens takes real pleasure in welcoming his guests and introducing them to the house he built with his own hands. Nevertheless, the presence of Mrs. Doumens can be found in the bouquets of dried flowers hanging from the beams, the colorfully embroidered plaids which liven up sofas and armchairs, and the choice of Provençal fabrics and quilted bedspreads. Everything else bears Mr. Doumens' stamp: the choice of a sleigh bed, doors from recycled wardrobes, the ceilings made of chestnut slats and colored planks, the sunny yellow and sienna hues, and even the homemade jams for breakfast: apricot, kiwi, and melon.

- 3 rooms: $55.
- 1 suite, sleeps 2/3: $85.
- Breakfast included.
- Open year round.

Castel Brando

Joëlle and Jean-Paul Pieri, 20222 Erbalunga. **Tel: 011 33 4 95 30 10 30.**
Fax: 011 33 4 95 33 98 18. www.castelbrando.com info@castelbrando.com

This magnificent *palazzu*, a 19th century mansion, opens its olive green shutters over a village palm grove. A large still-life enlivens the limewashed wall of the lounge. For the rooms, pine green is the color of choice, though a few have been done up in saffron-red, which echoes the small old hexagonal tiles on the floors. Early 20th century furniture, ancestral portraits on the stairway, and a typically Mediterranean *chiaroscuro* lifestyle underscore the charm of this inn. In the garden, the more contemporary looking "Villa Rose" suites include small terraces which open directly onto the pool.

- 19 rooms: $70–$140.
- 6 suites: $110–$165.
- Breakfast: $12.
- Pool.
- Closed from October 31 to March 15.

St-Clément-des-Baleines
St-Martin-de-Ré
Le Bois-Plage-en-Ré
LA ROCHELLE
NIORT
MONTMORILLON
MONTLUÇON
Allier
GUERET
VICHY
POITOU-CHARENTES
Vienne
BELLAC
AUVERGNE
ROCHEFORT
SAINT-JEAN-D'ANGELY
CONFOLENS
RIOM
LIMOGES
AUBUSSON
THIERS
Vars
SAINTES
COGNAC
Magnac-s-Touvre
ROCHECHOUART
CLERMONT-FERRAND
Charente
ANGOULEME
LIMOUSIN
USSEL
ISSOIRE
JONZAC
NONTRON
TULLE
LESPARRE-MEDOC
MAURIAC
BRIOUDE
BLAYE
BRIVE-LA-GAILLARDE
PERIGUEUX
SAINT-FLOUR
Lège-Cap-Ferret
Sourzac
SARLAT-LA-CANEDA
LIBOURNE
AURILLAC
BORDEAUX
BERGERAC
Lacave
GOURDON
Dordogne
Villeréal
FIGEAC
Lot
MENDE
LANGON
Garonne
Mercuès
VILLENEUVE-SUR-LOT
St-Cirq-Lapopie
AQUITAINE
CAHORS
Aveyron
RODEZ
VILLEFRANCHE-DE-ROUERGUE
AGEN
NERAC
MILLAU
MONT DE-MARSAN
CASTELSARRASIN
Donnazac
Midouze
CONDOM
MONTAUBAN
Tarn
Seignosse
Grenade-s-l'Adour
Saint-Puy
ALBI
Hossegor
DAX
Adour
MIDI-PYRENEES
AUCH
Mimbaste
BAYONNE
Adour
LODEVE
Bidart
Urcuit
St-Jean-de-Luz
TOULOUSE
Mirande
CASTRES
Sare
La Bastide-Clairence
Espelette
Monségur
Hérault
Poey-d'Oloron
PAU
MURET
BEZIERS
Fontrailles
Lasseube
OLORON-SAINTE-MARIE
CARCASSONNE
Aude
TARBES
SAINT-GAUDENS
Garonne
PAMIERS
NARBONNE
Accous
BAGNERES-DE-BIGORRE
LIMOUX
ARGELES-GAZOST
Beaucens
SAINT-GIRONS
FOIX
LANGUEDOC-ROUSSILLON
PERPIGNAN
PRADES
CERET
0
50
100 km

Southwest

Le Château de la Treyne
46200 Lacave.

La Pelissaria
46330 Saint-Cirq-Lapopie.

Le Mas Azémar
46090 Mercuès.

Les Vents Bleus
81170 Donnazac.

Le Chaufourg
24400 Sourzac.

Le Moulin de Labique
47210 Villeréal.

La Lumiane
32310 Saint Puy.

Le Moulin de Régis
32300 Mirande.

Les Musardises
65220 Fontrailles.

Eth Beyre Petit
65400 Beaucens.

La Ferme Dagué
64290 Lasseube.

Le Domaine de Pédelaborde
64400 Poey-d'Oloron.

L'Oustalet
64490 Accous.

Le Relais Linague
64990 Urcuit.

La Maison Sainbois
64240 La Bastide-Clairence.

La Croisade
64240 La Bastide-Clairence.

Olhabidea
64310 Sare.

La Maison Irigoïan
64210 Bidart.

Aretxola
64310 Sare.

Irazabala
64250 Espelette.

La Devinière
64500 Saint-Jean-de-Luz.

Maison Cap Blanc
64460 Monségur.

Pain, Adour et Fantaisie
40270 Grenade-sur-l'Adour.

Capcazal de Pachiou
40350 Mimbaste.

Ty Gias
40510 Seignosse.

Les Hortensias du Lac
40150 Hossegor.

La Maison du Bassin
33970 Lège-Cap-Ferret.

L'Hôtel de l'Océan
17580 Le Bois-Plage-en-Ré.

Le Chat Botté
17590 Saint-Clément-des-Baleines.

La Maison Douce
17410 Saint-Martin-de-Ré.

Le Château de Maumont
16600 Magnac-sur-Touvre.

Le Logis du Portal
16330 Vars.

Le Château de la Treyne

Michèle Gombert, 46200 Lacave. **Tel: 011 33 5 65 27 60 60.**
Fax: 011 33 5 65 27 60 70. www.chateaudelatreyne.com contact@chateaudelatreyne.com

From the terrace at la Treyne, you'll marvel at the sheer views over the Dordogne river. Surrounded by vast French-style gardens, the castle's oldest stones date back to the 14th century. The old alcoves, like the Louis XVI room, still have their faithful guests, but the latest rooms, with terraces over the river, already have their fans, too, because of their idyllic location alone. But don't overlook the remaining rooms: "Soleil Levant" or "Rising Sun," with its madras cottons, is installed in the former chapel; "Duc," with a view of the bend in the river; "Tour," with its sweeping frescoes; and "Cardinale," with its open timberwork. And be don't surprised if, at dusk, you find yourself, champagne glass in hand, relaxing in one of the cozy lounges.

- 11 rooms: $170–$460.
- 4 suites: $580.
- Breakfast: $17.
- Menus: $45–$100.
- Pool, tennis.
- Closed from November 15 to November 30, and from January to Easter.

La Pelissaria Lot

46330 Saint-Cirq-Lapopie. **Tel: 011 33 5 65 31 25 14. Fax: 011 33 5 65 30 25 52.**
www.quercy.net/com/pelissaria lapelissariahotel@minitel.net

This old abode, straddling one of the rocky escarpments which survey the Lot river, is located in a village which is among "the most beautiful in France." The terraces of La Pelissaria offer one of the prettiest views over a cascade of roofs the color of singed bread. It is a real treat to take an early breakfast and contemplate the sunrise as it skims the river, then the gilded stone of the medieval buildings. Nights are quiet in the bedrooms decorated with regional furniture and wrought iron artwork made by a village craftsman.

- 8 rooms: $75–$115.
- 2 suites: $120.
- Breakfast: $10.
- Pool.
- Closed from November to April.

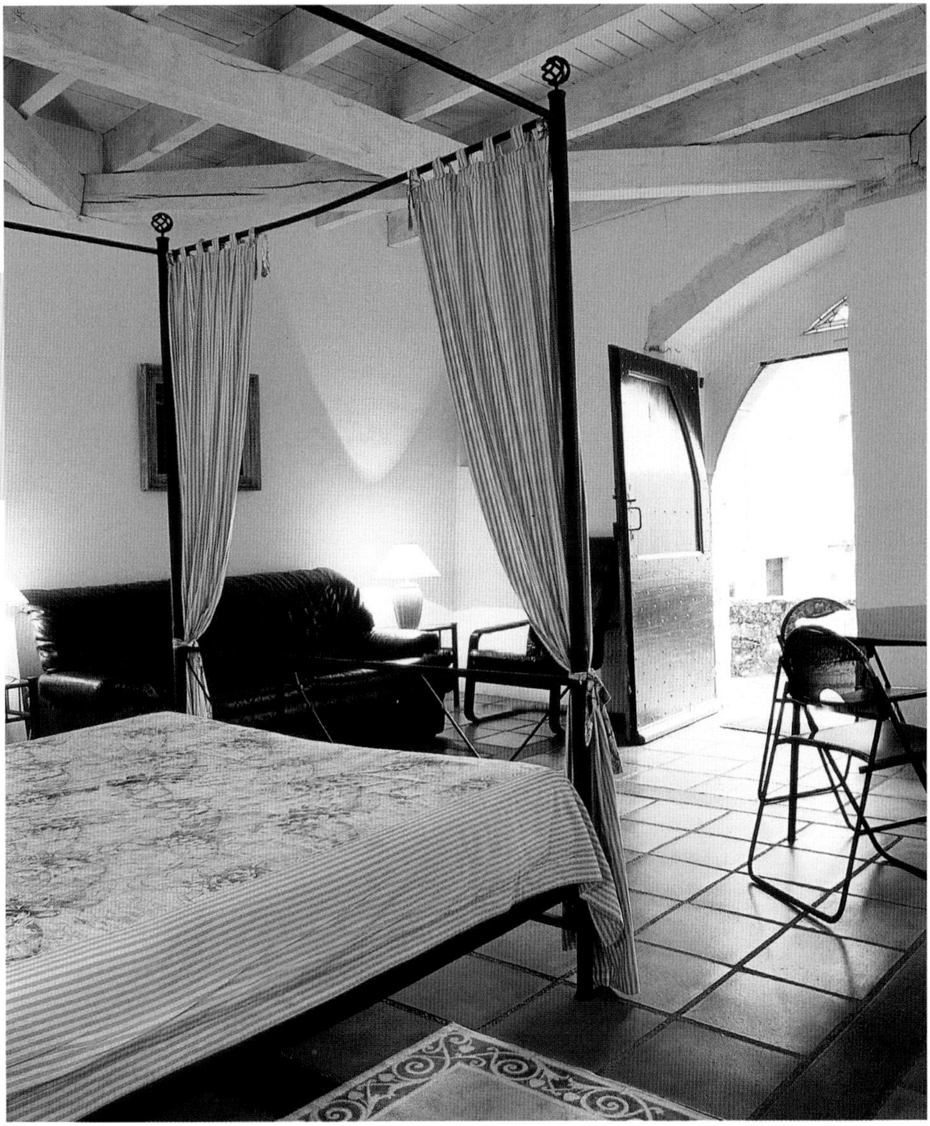

Le Mas Azémar

Rue du Mas de Vinssou, 46090 Mercuès. **Tel: 011 33 5 65 30 96 85.**
Fax: 011 33 5 65 30 53 82. www.masazemar.com masazemar@aol.com

At the foot of the Mercuès vineyards, you get to this farmhouse through a large courtyard surrounded by outbuildings. The main thing here is light. Without detracting from the elegant rusticity of the place, light pierces the large yellow living room opening onto the garden, and becomes more filtered in the kitchen, where superb stone work has been exposed. Logs crackle beneath the mantle piece. This is where you will sample regional dishes and home-cooking. The rooms vie to seduce you with their stone walls scrubbed bare, painted in blue, yellow, and green stripes, their old-style beds, toile de Jouy, and Provençal knickknacks. Throughout, rediscovered portraits of the inn's forebears watch over the rooms—a blessing to the future of this place that was brought to life by a photographer who's since fallen in love with the winding landscapes of the Lot.

- 6 rooms: $70–$80.
- Breakfast included.
- Meals: $30.
- Pool.
- Open year round.
- No pets allowed.

Les Vents Bleus

Tarn

Isabelle and Laurent Philibert, Route de Caussade, 81170 Donnazac.
Tel/fax: 011 33 5 63 56 86 11. lesventsbleus@free.fr

This 18th century mansion, roofed with rounded tiles, is awash in the scent of fig trees. Here, Isabelle and Laurent Philibert have prepared four bedrooms and a suite with refined decor, tempered by soft-hued fabrics in lavender or powder blue, white on white, buttercup, and striped vermilion. Beneath the open beams, the walls are of stone scrubbed bare, rooms sports regional knickknacks, Indian screens, and Oriental lights—all confirming the southerly flavor of the place. And beneath white parasols and wooden awnings, Isabelle serves food that is original, gourmet, and plentiful.

- 4 rooms and 1 suite: $75–$130.
- Breakfast included.
- Meals: $30.
- Pool.
- Open year round.
- No pets allowed.

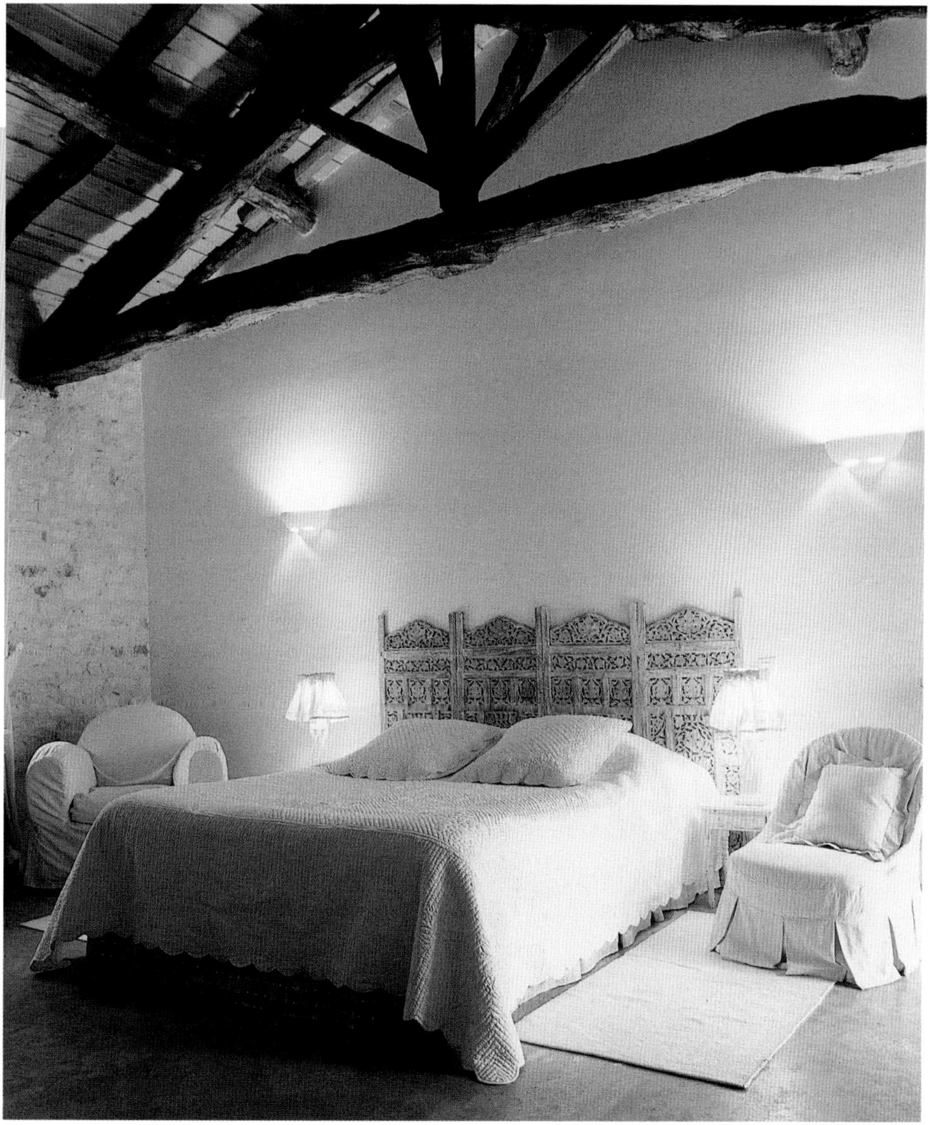

Dordogne

Le Chaufourg

Georges Dambier, 24400 Sourzac. **Tel: 011 33 5 53 81 01 56.**
Fax: 011 33 5 53 82 94 87. chaufourg.hotel@wanadoo.fr

For Georges Dambier, Le Chaufourg was above all a boyhood house, which he left as a teenager to travel the world. Today this hamlet of mossy stones is open for passing guests. With its walls and roofs the color of amber and scorched bread, the property belong to this Isle, which has an ambience all its own. Le Chaufourg offers a range of lounges and bedrooms dominated by white and ivory. Just a dash of blue as a highlight here and there, and tobacco for the music room. In one of the suites, a bull's-eye window, integrated into the bed's headboard, reveals the grounds and their greenery. Things literary and things country are both at home in this bucolic setting. Even though modern comfort is everywhere, all the rooms preserve the soul of yesterday, as well.

- 5 rooms: $145–$240.
- 4 suites: starting at $275.
- Breakfast: $17.
- Dinner: $35–$55.
- Pool.
- Closed from November 15 to March 15.

Le Moulin de Labique

Saint-Eutrope-de-Born, 47210 Villeréal. **Tel: 011 33 5 53 01 63 90.**
Fax: 011 33 5 53 01 73 17. moulin-de-labique@wanadoo.fr

With its verandah built on stone pillars, this beautiful 18th century building has a slightly colonial air, Tuscany gone astray. Yet we're in the heart of the Lot-et-Garonne, and everything is steeped in the easy life: the Impressionist garden, the mirror-like waters of the Lagardonne, the rooms clad in floral fabrics, with grass-green and chick-yellow hues softening the sober effect of the terra-cotta floors. Watercolors, fading old color prints, family pictures galore, and splendid country wardrobes fill this place. A stairway in peacock-blue ironwork leads to two other English-style rooms, while a plum-colored suite leads to its own private terrace. A dining room has been set up in the former sharecropper's house, offering food much inspired by the southwest.

- 4 rooms: $90.
- 2 suites: $135.
- Breakfast included.
- Meals: starting at $25.
- Pool, horseback riding.
- Open year round.

La Lumiane

Jean-Louis and Catherine Scarantino, Grande-Rue, 32310 Saint-Puy.
Tel: 011 33 5 62 28 95 95. Fax: 011 33 5 62 28 59 67. la.lumiane@wanadoo.fr

One morning, while on vacation, Catherine Scarantino was stopped short by a photo of ruins displayed in the window of a realtor. She visited, and refused to leave. Today, owners Jean-Louis and Catherine have fallen in love with La Lumiane, an 18th century house adjoining a 12th century church. The main building opens onto a garden, and a beautiful 18th century stone stairway leads to the pastel-hued rooms. White and soft blue for "Glycines," with its balcony looking over a large swimming pool. A garland of flowers with entwined cupids for "des Roses;" a 19th century feel for "Tilleuls;" and for "des Vignes," which is installed in an outbuilding, blueish fabrics. Terra-cotta floors, tinted woodwork, and a dining-room with open beams have all helped to preserve the rustic nobility of this dwelling.

- 5 rooms: $65.
- Little cottage with 2 rooms: $615 for a week.
- Breakfast included.
- Meals: $25.
- Pool.
- Open year round.

Le Moulin de Régis

Gers

Gisèle and Pierre Trémont, 32300 Mirande.
Tel/fax: 011 33 5 62 66 51 06.

In the 14th century this building, festooned with hydrangeas and encircled by a wrought iron verandah, used to be the mill of Astarac Castle. As a boy, Pierre Trémont would come and play here amid sacks of corn, fascinated by the miller's activities. In 1972, he purchased the mill and began restoring it. He repaired the machinery and played the part of miller. As for his wife, Gisèle, she fell passionately for her new house. With the help of the best craftsmen in the area, she had the walls plastered and given an old-style finish. A veritable celebration of colors, enhanced by large, Spanish-type shawls hung over the gallery of the inner courtyard, helped the inn take on a gypsy-like mood. Add to that Provençal quilted bedspreads scattered with bright-colored flowers, and country patchworks tossed over the beds, and the scene is set. Breakfast, with generous platters of local cold cuts, is served on farm tables covered with starched linen cloths.

- 6 rooms: $90.
- Breakfast included.
- 1 cottage, sleeps 5: $800 for a week.
- Indoor pool.
- Open year round.

Les Musardises

Mrs. Casteret, 65220 Fontrailles.
Tel: 011 33 5 62 35 51 70.

A beautiful façade with red shutters opens onto an array of meadows and fields. All the rooms in this country inn are dedicated to music and opera, the passion of the lady of the house. "Arabella," the most seductive of them, fills a ground-floor wing.

- Rooms: $65.
- Breakfast included.
- Menus: $25.
- Open year round.

Light and shadows mingle here in a slightly Oriental atmosphere, honey and slate hues dominate the color scheme, complementing a crocheted ivory bedspread. Through a large picture window in the simple bathroom you'll spy a secret garden. Two other rooms, both with more country atmospheres but no less imaginative, share the upper floor.

Eth Beyre Petit

Mrs. Vielle, 15 route de Vielle, 65400 Beaucens.
Tel/fax: 011 33 5 62 97 90 02. contact@beyrepetit.com

This is a blue house with a roof that resembles a nun's headdress, overlooking the Viscos, one of the symbolic peaks of the Pyrenees. It has belonged to the same family since the 9th century, invariably handed down to the eldest son. The door key, dated to 1790, still opens the front door. In the spare but cozy living room, a fire simmers in the hearth, flanked by berry-red banquettes. An 18th century walnut stairway leads to the rooms—all with views over the mountains. In "La Galerie," you'll find Napoleon III furniture, offset by quilted white cotton with pink hems on a green background. And the twin rooms on the second floor, with patchwork quilts, and toile de Jouy and floral fabrics, are as romantic as you can get.

- 3 rooms: $45–$60.
- Breakfast included.
- Meals: $15.
- Open year round.

La Ferme Dagué

Jean-Pierre Maumus, Chemin Croix-de-Dagué, 64290 Lasseube.
Tel/fax: 011 33 5 59 04 27 11.

On the old Compostela pilgrimage routes, nestled into the foothills of the Pyrenees, this farm is typical of those which populated the Jurançon hillsides. Behind its porch, an enclosed courtyard surrounded by a wooden gallery and flanked by a passageway with slates at least 300 years old speaks to the property's history. The former chicken run and the pigpens still have their original chestnut latticework. And behind this façade, a couple of young mountain folk who offer a truly warm welcome, have opened up five guest rooms. The interior decor, with its sheafs of reeds scattered haphazardly on landings, its pictures of leaves and grasses, and its old hayracks acting as headboards, respects an authentic setting cleverly adapted to the here and now.

- 4 rooms: $55.
- 1 suite: $85.
- 1 room sleeps 4: $80.
- Breakfast included.
- Open year round.

Le Domaine de Pédelaborde

Mr. and Mrs. Civit, 64400 Poey-d'Oloron. **Tel/fax: 011 33 5 59 39 59 93.**
http://perso.wanadoo.fr/civit/ civit.earl@wanadoo.fr

In the midst of a working farm, this 18th century family house, once only used in the summer, has rooms arranged around a traditional Béarn enclosed courtyard. Named after different valleys—Ossau, Aubisque, Somport, and Aspe—the rooms are seductive in deep blue perked up by peony pinks. They all express the art of living well without giving in to showiness, with beautiful swathes of exotic birds, orange-colored madras, and corn-yellow tones. In the bathrooms, the Béarn towels add a distinctive touch and breakfast is a real treat, offering a generous array of homemade cakes. And for those who linger longer? The prospect of sampling the farm's homegrown foie gras three times throughout the week (fresh, cooked, and semi-cooked)!

- 4 rooms: $40–$50.
- Breakfast included.
- Dinner: $18.
- Pool.
- Open year round.

L'Oustalet

Christine Bruno, 64490 Accous.
Tel/fax: 011 33 5 59 34 74 39.

The mountain looming over it has certainly influenced the character of this medieval house in the heart of a small, picturesque town, just beneath the crags of the Isseye. A bed of river pebbles leads to a door made from a picture window. A combination of mountain rusticity and contemporary austerity is on hand here, from broad chestnut planks, panels of bare granite, and age-old woodwork to paneling, soft shades of ivory, and creamy pastels. The verdict? This inn has managed to adapt to time passing without losing its soul. The Béarn linen fabric covering the old sofa in the lounge is signature enough of the identity of the area. Add to it a friendly welcome and nearby paths, where you can take walks and hikes, and this is a great retreat.

- 3 rooms: $55–$70.
- Breakfast included.
- Open year round.

Le Relais Linague

Marie Bléau, chemin Linague, 64990 Urcuit.
Tel/fax: 011 33 5 59 42 97 97.

Just a few seasons ago, trees were growing here in the midst of the ruins of a 17th century house. Today this is one of the prettiest addresses around. It's a dwelling full of light and tranquillity, dominated by nature and spring colors. Abandoned chestnut timber, old shutters which have been put back into service as picture frames, a stone sink turned into a dresser—innkeeper Marie Bléau's house is full of surprises. Here, a collection of old hats and lace nightshirts cover a wall; there, roses on top of a wardrobe look down onto a bed covered in ivory goffered cloth. You just never know what you'll come across next.

- 5 rooms: $60–$65.
- Breakfast included.

La Maison Sainbois

Colette Haramboure, 64240 La Bastide-Clairence. **Tel: 011 33 5 59 29 54 20.**
Fax: 011 33 5 59 29 55 42. www.sainbois.fr sainbois@aol.com

- 4 rooms: $60–$75.
- 1 suite: $85–$95.
- Breakfast: $6–$10.
- Meals: $25.
- Pool.
- Open year round.

When a country house succeeds in balancing tradition and modernity, perfection is close at hand. This is the case with the Maison Sainbois. Behind its deep-red timberwork facade, most of the inn's rooms have been repainted dove gray. When it's a cloudy day on the slopes of the Pyrenees, a flame in the fireplace highlights the beautiful stone slabs of the ground floor. And it's in this stylish room where Colette Haramboure, a wine expert, treats her guests to regional creations. The rooms take their names from Basque provinces: "Souletine" features a blend of blues set off by delightful old prints; "Guipuzcoa," with its brick-red ginghams and silken Indian fabrics, has a balcony overlooking a swimming pool and a teak deck. "Biscaye," in golden brown and dark purple, is elegant; while "Navarre," with splashes of buttercup and Arcangues blue, is cheerful. And "Labourdine" accommodates families in a suite where country-green tiles go with caramel ginghams.

La Croisade

Mrs. Darritchon, 64240 La Bastide-Clairence.
Tel: 011 33 5 59 29 68 22. Fax: 011 33 5 59 29 62 99. sylvianeD@aol.com

On nice days, you'll relax in the garden shaded by lemon trees and oleander. But when a cloudy day sends you inside, you'll equally enjoy the warmth of this old staging post-turned-inn on the road to Compostela. Done in bursts of vivid colors, such as the beautiful kilim used to soften footsteps on the old cement tiles, La Croisade has a distinct personality. A beautiful oak staircase rounded with age leads to a small landing where family pictures offer a sense of intimacy and French windows open onto a small balcony entwined with Virginia creeper. The rooms underscore the romance of the inn: "Cordoue," a bit Indian, a bit Moroccan, exudes a worldly flair; "Séville" is like a tangy sweet; while the decoration of "Pampelune" seems to have come straight out of a candy box, with two cherubs framing a knotted organza canopy over the bed.

- 4 rooms and 1 suite: $55–$65.
- Breakfast included.
- Meals: $20.
- Open year round.

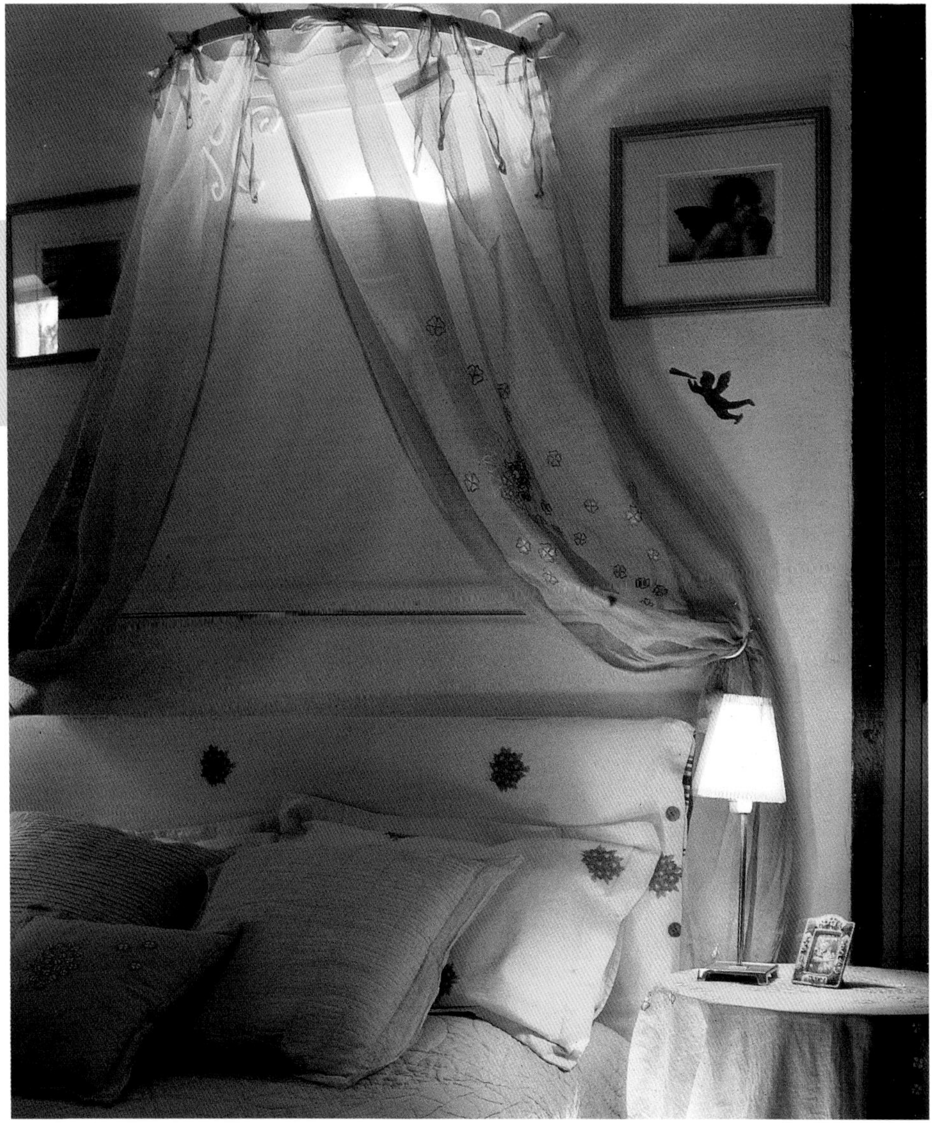

Olhabidea

Anne-Marie Fagoaga, 64310 Sare. **Tel: 011 33 5 59 54 21 85.**
Fax: 011 33 5 59 47 50 41. www.basquexplorer.com/olhabidea.

Set among meadows, Olhabidea isn't far from the picturesque village of Sare, right in the Basque country. Owner Anne-Marie Fagoaga presides over this rustic guest house—especially its kitchen, where you might find rice pudding gurgling on the stove, heralding breakfast. In the big entry hall the tiles gleam with wax, and bedrooms are filled with timber furniture, typical for a country inn of this region. But what sets this place apart from the rest is the individuality of its decor. Each room features a mix of themes: florals and tartans, stripes, polka dots and ginghams, powder blue and caramel. Offbeat, yet completely in tune with the rustic mood of the place.

- 5 rooms: $55–$65.
- 1 suite: $110.
- Breakfast included.
- Closed from November 1 to March 30.

La Maison Irigoïan

Philippe Etcheverry, avenue de Biarritz. 64210 Bidart. **Tel: 011 33 5 59 43 83 00.**
Fax: 011 33 5 59 43 83 03. www.irigoian.com irigoian@wanadoo.fr

Just a stone's throw from the sea, Irigoïan's blue shutters open onto a garden filled with hydrangeas, adjoining the Ilbarritz golf course. Philippe Etcheverry, mindful of tradition, kept the farm's name—which means "above the village"—a village that happens to be among the oldest along the coast. Uninhabited for close to 40 years, the house has remained virtually unchanged. Today, Philippe has restored everything. Five bedrooms, spacious and clean, are installed in the old lofts. Anise, soft blue, oleander, buttercup, and brown have pepped up the paneling, matching the frieze of *azulejos* tiles that line the steps of the staircase. Terra-cotta floors, linen drapes, traditional flooring, and passageways hung with lithographs by Basque painter Monzon Uria complete the look.

- 5 rooms: starting at $75.
- Breakfast: $8.
- Weekend or weekly fixed rates for golf and seawater therapy.
- Open year round.

Aretxola

Mrs. Trini Devaucoux, Route des Grottes, 64310 Sare.
Tel: 011 33 5 59 54 21 85.

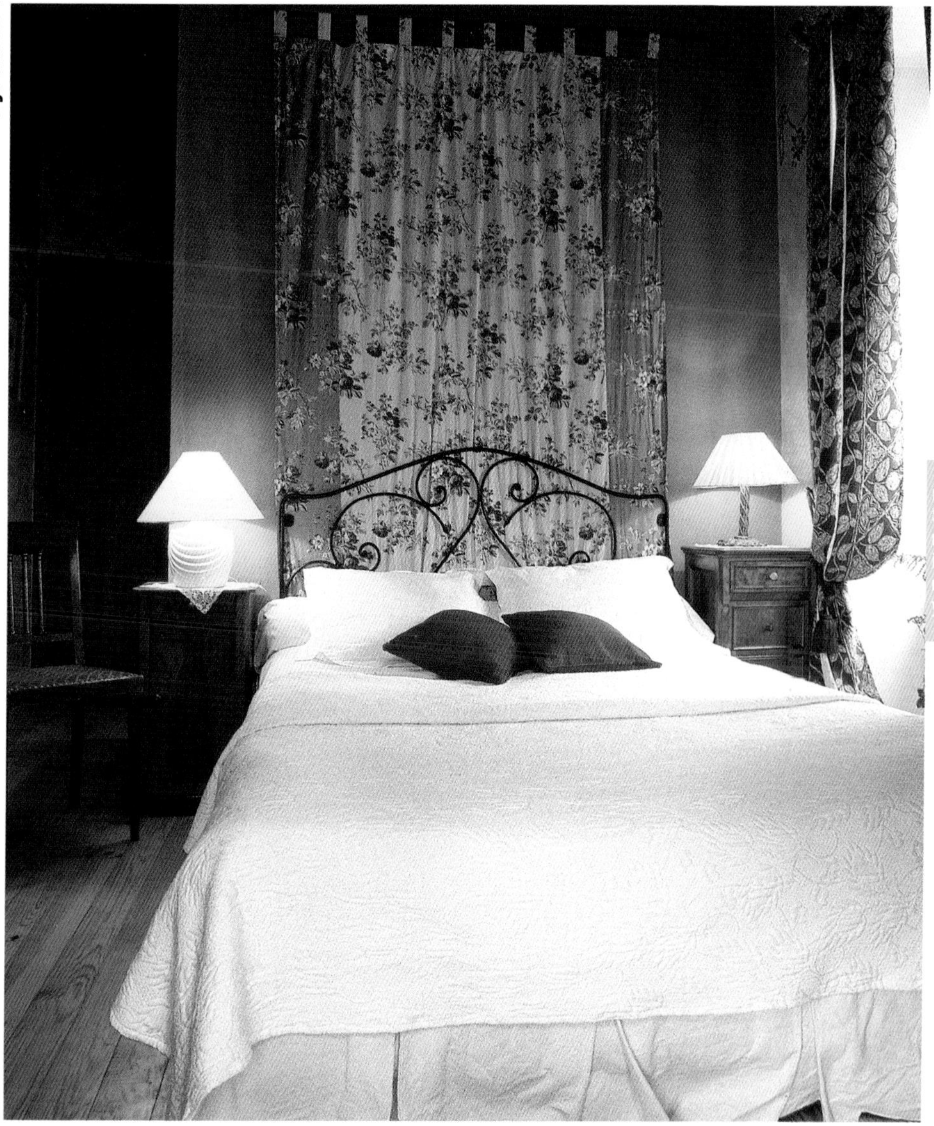

Behind its green shutters, this former farmhouse contains two rooms, both with a country feel. One is hung with an antique cloth covered in roses, and sports coral-pink linen in the bathroom. Its terrace leads to the garden on the same level. The second room, situated in the old hay loft, has a fusion of bluish tones with slate-gray toile de Jouy, ginghams, and local hydrangeas. A marriage screen serves as a headboard, and a frieze of wisteria leads from the dressing room to the balcony. The dining room still has its original paving stones, but the centerpiece is the old wood-framed trolley, which is laden with the makings of a fine country breakfast.

- 2 rooms: $50–$60.
- Breakfast included.
- Open year round.

Irazabala

Sylvie Toffolo-Fagoaga, 155 Mendiko Bidea, 64250 Espelette.
Tel: 011 33 5 59 93 02. Fax: 011 33 5 59 93 80 18. kanbil@wanadoo.fr

This half-timbered house so typical of the area owes its name to the long path, edged with ferns, that leads to it. At the top of the hill, there's a 360 degree view of the Pyrenees and its pastoral hillsides. Innkeeper Sylvie Toffolo-Fagoaga and her husband chose to live here in this ancestral home, where, under the same roof, three generations co-exist in harmony. In the entrance hall, where pigs, chickens, and cows were once kept, sits the great-grandmother's carved marriage chest. On the second floor, two rooms are shaded by red- or blue-checkered drapes. There's a canopy of muslin and pictures of roses for "Artzamendia" ('Bear's Mountain"), embroidered linen and forget-me-not gingham for "Baigura," which takes its name from another Pyrenean summit.

- 2 rooms: $60–$80.
- Breakfast included.
- Open year round.

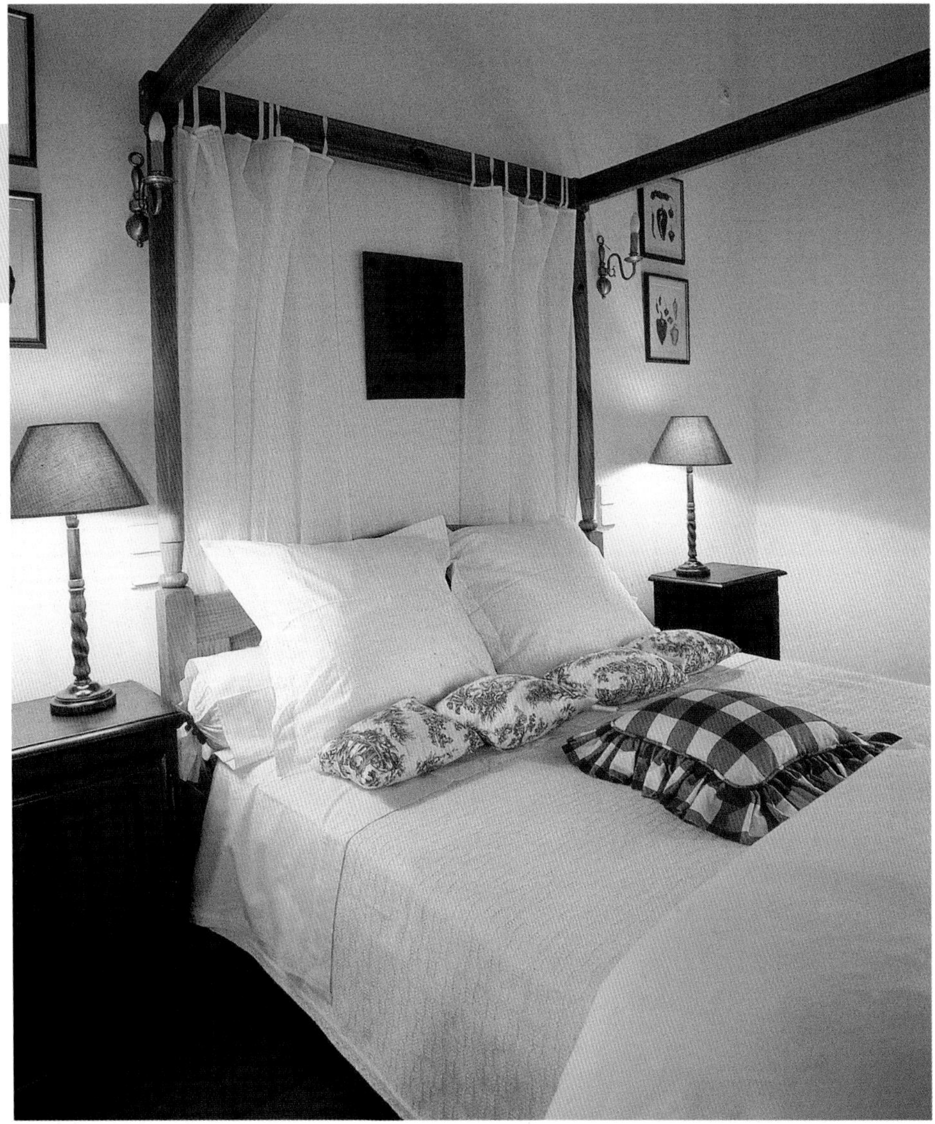

Pyrénées-Atlantiques

La Devinière

Marie-France and Bernard Carrère, 5, rue Loquin, 64500 Saint-Jean-de-Luz.
Tel: 011 33 5 59 26 05 51. Fax: 011 33 5 59 51 26 38.

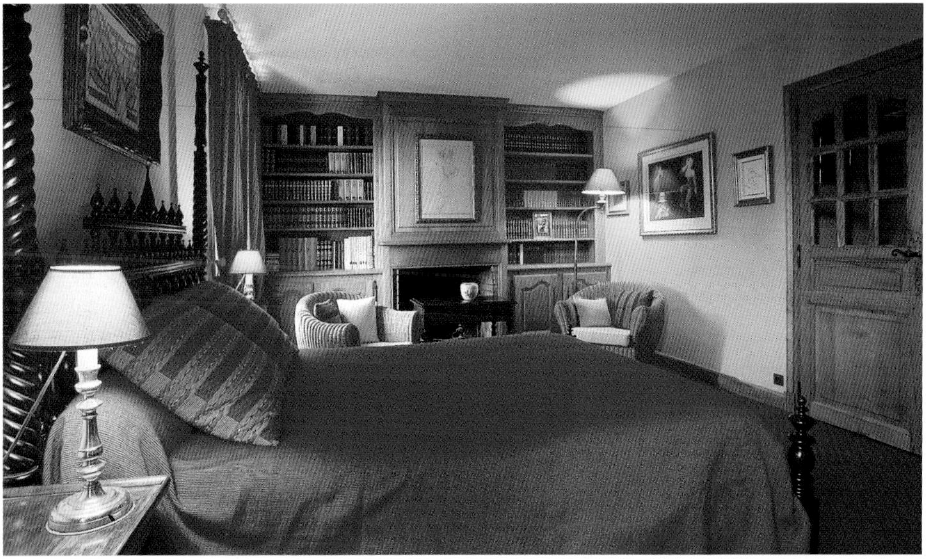

In the heart of Saint-Jean-de-Luz, the owners of this superb Basque house have realized their lifelong dream. With its romantic, cozy atmosphere, its patiently chosen antique furniture and flea-markets finds (bronzes, statues, and knickknacks picked up by following the heart and the seasons), Marie-France and Bernard Carrère have given this family home a lot of thought. Ten bedrooms wind around a chestnut staircase, and you can see their fondness for gentle country atmospheres in each one. Done up in dusty pinks, soft yellows, cashmere in shades of blue, and warm woodwork, each is warmer than the next. Flowers from the garden are placed in the rooms, and come winter, head to the crackling fireplace to savor the warmth that's certainly an ongoing theme here.

- 10 rooms: $110–$150.
- Breakfast: $12.
- Open year round.

Maison Cap Blanc

Francine Maumy, 64460 Monségur.
Tel: 011 33 5 59 81 54 52. maumy.francine@wanadoo.fr

The walls jump to life in shades of ochre, yellow, orange, lime, anise, and turquoise. Pottery, table mats emblazoned with roosters or hens, and glasses in nests of white ironwork or chicken wire all lend to the rural ambience here. Roosters, this time in the guise of door stops, punctuate some rooms, where you can still see walls in woven timber work held together by their cob—a mixture of clay and straw. A branch of a tree supports the headboard of the "Sunflower" room. "Liberty" boasts a cloth canopy in a combination of small, red checks and repeated floral patterns. And warmed by a small blue eiderdown quilt with yellow flowers and assorted bows, "Violette" could be the sweetest room of all.

- 4 rooms: $60–$70.
- Additional bed: $20.
- Breakfast included.
- Meals: $20.
- Pool.
- Open year round.

Pain, Adour et Fantaisie

14-16, place des Tilleuls, 40270 Grenade-sur-l'Adour.
Tel: 011 33 5 58 45 18 80. Fax: 011 33 5 58 45 16 57.

Away from the seashore and the coastal pinewood, the land of Gascony has become synonymous with good food. And at the foot of the river Adour is this small hotel—the place to pass a summer's evening, relaxing on its candle-lit terrace. Dinner, courtesy of chef Philippe Garret, will no doubt be an inventive dish with a blend of Atlantic and Mediterranean influences. The hotel has just under a dozen rooms divided between two large 17th and 18th century manor houses, and most of them have a terrace or a balcony overlooking the Adour. They're all done in clear water and vanilla tones. A favorite? The one overlooking the street, the "Retour du Nil"—"Return to the Nile"—for its harmonious blend of seagreen and its Empire style.

■ 11 rooms: $70–$130.
■ Breakfast: $13.
■ Menus: $30.
■ Closed one week in December and one week in February.

Capcazal de Pachiou

Landes

Colette Alberca-Dufourcet, 40350 Mimbaste.
Tel/fax: 011 33 5 58 55 30 54.

In the small valleys of the Chalosse, on the border between the Landes and the Béarn, and not very far away from the Compostela pilgrimage route, you'll find Capcazal de Pachiou. The home dates back 500 years, and innkeeper Colette Alberca-Dufourcet has put all her energy and finances into restoring the place. Rich in interesting objects, such as the aviary cage that hangs above two clocks, the inn charms with its eccentricities and history. Consider the Balcony Room, draped in toile de Jouy, and designed expressly for a wedding night in the year... 1756! And the "Jeannette" suite, which occupies the site where the maids' rooms used to be.

- 3 rooms and 1 suite: $50–$65.
- Meals: $20.
- Open year round.

Ty Gias

Noëllie Annic, 1, avenue Hilton Head, 40510 Seignosse. **Tel/fax: 011 33 5 58 41 64 29.**
http://perso.wanadoo.fr/tygias tygias@wanadoo.fr

Noëllie Annic dreamed of a house with different levels, covered by a multitude of roofs, built on planks. An architect helped her realize her dream. Her house is set below a crowd of pine trees, in the middle of a garden. You navigate from one room to another—or, rather, from one "deck" to another—on gangways of wood, between walls of blue boards. Picture windows let in a profusion of light. A separate building, which has the fresh scent of raw wood, houses rooms decorated with bluish comforters and large linen sheets. The rooms are preceded by a small lounge with powdered white planks, and connected to shower rooms fashioned like beach cabins. A private garden completes the California-inspired motif. Next to the swimming pool, there's a terrace where brunch is served.

- 2 rooms: $55–$75.
- 1 suite: $110–$140.
- Breakfast included.
- Pool.
- Open year round.

Les Hortensias du Lac

1578, avenue du Tour du Lac, 40150 Hossegor.
Tel: 011 33 5 58 43 99 00. Fax: 011 33 5 58 43 42 81.

There's a nostalgic 1930s feel to this small hotel, and a look that recalls the lake and sunny vacations. Recently renovated from top to bottom by a young team who knew how to hold on to the charm of the Belle Epoque, this Basques/Landes hotel, with 24 rooms and suites, is tucked away behind a nest of hydrangeas. The decor is gray, white, and blue, set off by soft carpets spangled with starfish, blue plaids, and silvery lamps. From the picture window, you can see the garden, which has direct access to the beach. Four-poster beds with brown and slate-gray striped throws, bluish quilted bedspreads, bowls full of pine cones, furniture made of polished teak, and volcanic stones lend the rooms a decidedly contemporary look.

- 11 rooms: $90–$155.
- 8 duplexes: $110–$180.
- 5 suites: $110–$330.
- Breakfast buffet with champagne: $17.
- Closed from November 6 to March 31.

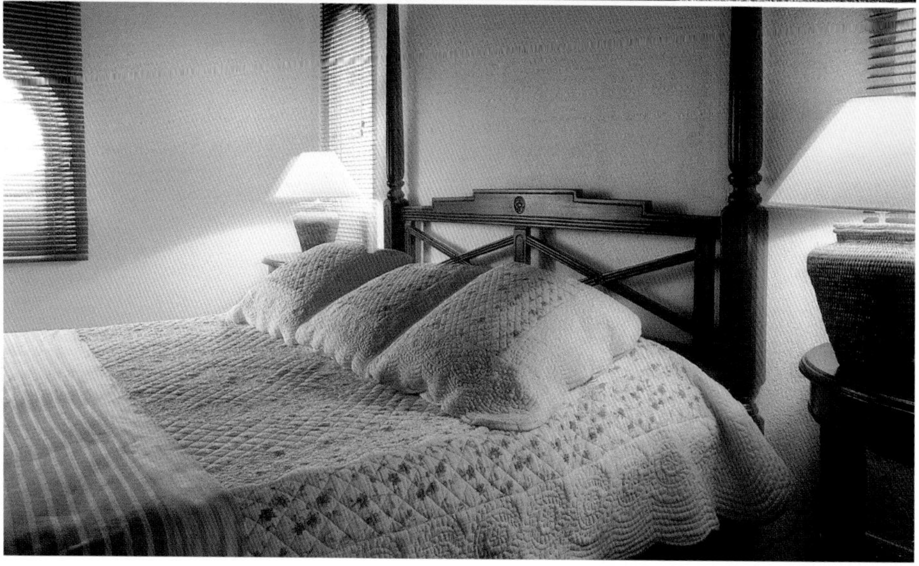

La Maison du Bassin

5, rue des Pionniers, 33970 Lège-Cap-Ferret.
Tel: 011 33 5 56 60 60 63. Fax: 011 33 5 56 03 71 47.

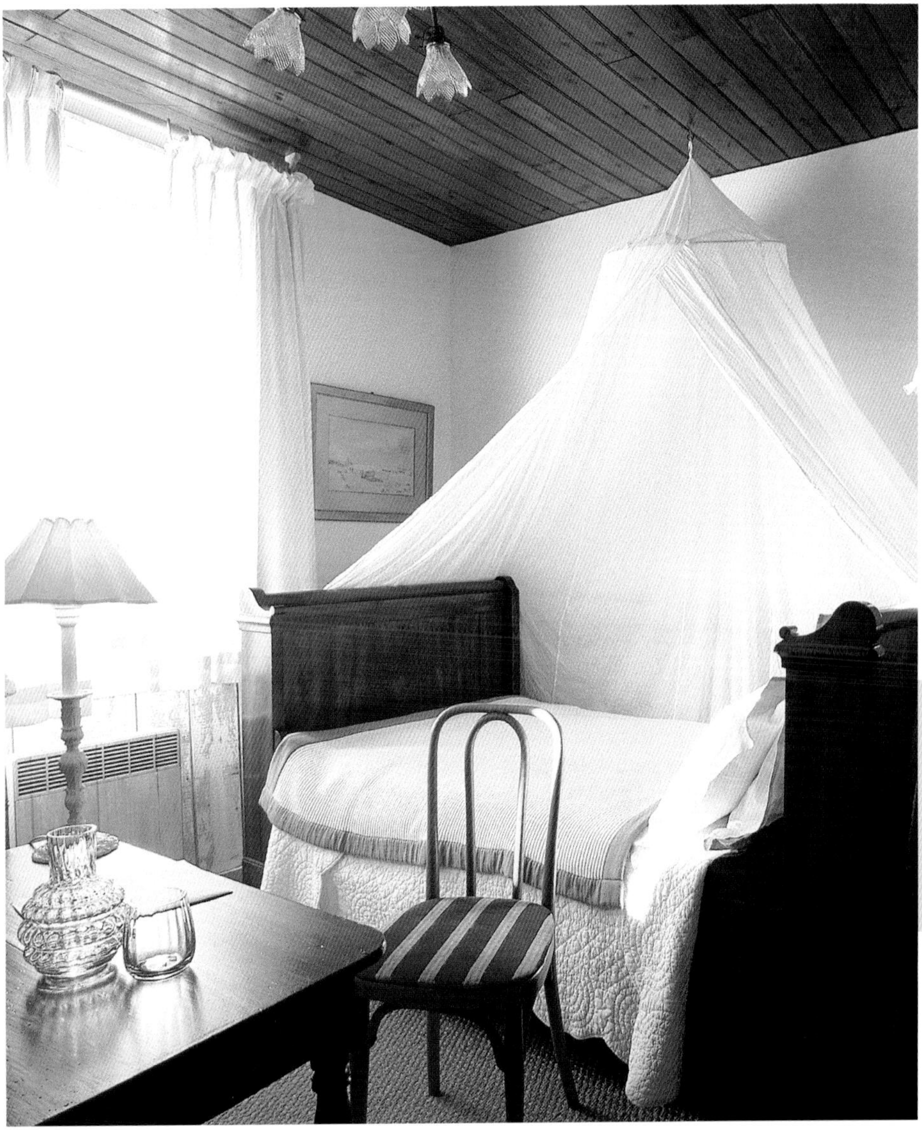

Time-honored base of a summer season at Cap-Ferret, a while back, the former Hôtel de Bayonne went in for a facelift, and came out as La Maison du Bassin. From then on, the shell-shaped key rings have opened the door to friendly intimacies—sometimes with the ocean, sometimes with its bar, full of juicy stories. Whether they look like cabins on an ocean liner, or sea side bungalows, whether they dream in white or blue, the color of the Atlantic, of surf swept lagoons or Venetian blinds, the color of vanilla, between pitch pine furniture and linen drapes, retro seascapes or driftwood, these rooms have the nostalgia of stopovers filled with the scent of ylang-ylang and big white lilies. Coir matting on which we quietly glide, carries the residents away, in the wake of sleeping flotsam, toward the chestnut armchairs dancing in circles round the sideboards in the dining room. The night bar, moored alongside the terrace, stretches out the summer evenings around a rum drink, all ready for nursing, and a sofa with a coppery glow.

- 7 rooms: $80–$120.
- 2 suites: $200.
- Breakfast: $12.
- Meals: $35.
- Closed in January and February.

L'Hôtel de l'Océan

172, rue Saint-Martin, 17580 Le Bois-Plage-en-Ré. **Tel: 011 33 5 46 09 23 07.**
Fax: 011 33 5 46 09 05 40. www.re-hotel-ocean.com contact@re-hotel-ocean.com

Behind green shutters and coats of whitewash, several country houses have united to create an "ocean" of serenity. This ocean shelters about 20 rooms that bask in the sea air. They're decorated with Atlantic tiles, quilted bedspreads, storm-blue drapes printed with silky flowers, and embroidered sheets trimmed with tartan. There's stripped furniture, Indian chiffonniers with a slate-gray finish, mirrors framed with driftwood, and shower rooms that make you feel as though you're bathing on the deck of a boat. In the reading room, funny old armchairs are planted on a sisal carpet, and the restaurant, in a large room with a low ceiling—typical of the island—is decorated with pictures of boats. Around the tables you'll find gourmets who love the fresh seafood and other seasonal delights served here. On beautiful days, they settle down on the terrace to await their maritime feast.

- 24 rooms: $60–$95.
- Breakfast: $10.
- Half-board: starting at $60.
- Closed from January 5 to February 5.

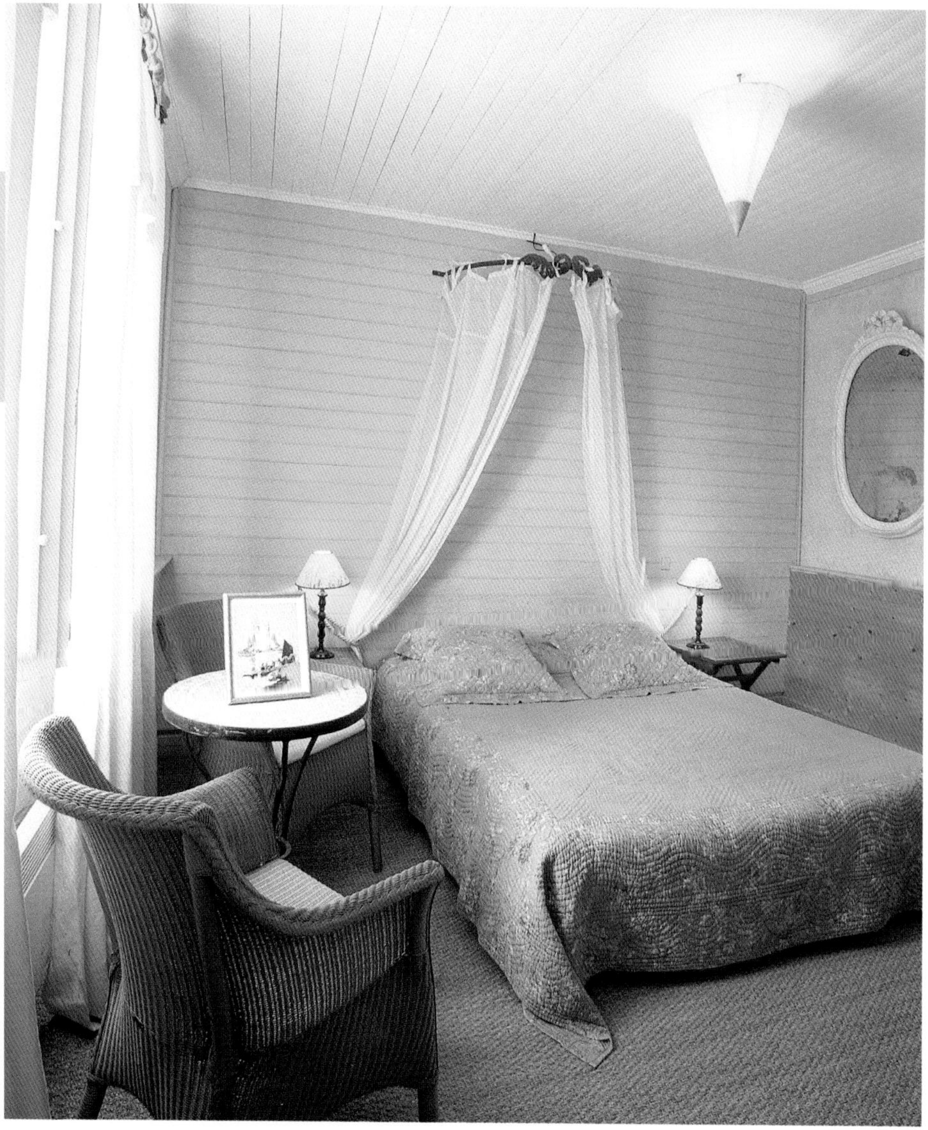

Le Chat Botté

Place de l'Eglise, 17590 Saint-Clément-des-Baleines.
Tel: 011 33 5 46 29 21 93. Fax: 011 33 5 46 29 29 97. www.lechatbotte.com

This small, 19-room hotel, done in pinkish and milky-cream hues and enhanced with fabrics inspired by the ocean or the sun, has taken on the personality of the island it calls home. Decorated with an array of quilted bedspreads, linen sheets, and rustic and Art Deco furniture, Le Chat Botté is a true retreat. Coir rugs, armchairs in chestnut, and painted paneling are the hallmarks of this place heavily influenced by the gentleness of the islands. The breakfast lounge/ verandah suits the country ambience perfectly, with its sheaves of rushes, its sitting hens, its pine wreaths, its tables covered with long linen cloths, its chubby armchairs, and its ample, paunchy sofas.

- 19 rooms: $65–$110.
- Breakfast: $10.
- Meals: $25.
- Spa.
- Closed from December 1 to December 15, and from January 6 to February 12.

La Maison Douce

Mr. and Mrs. Brunel, 25, rue Mérindot, 17410 Saint-Martin-de-Ré. **Tel: 011 33 5 46 09 20 20.**
Fax: 011 33 5 49 09 09 90. www.lamaisondouce.com maisondouce@iledere.com

Like a jealously guarded secret between the high walls of Saint-Martin-de-Ré, this inn is hidden 330 yards from the port, blending into the silvery-gray of the neighboring marshes. Located in a 19th century home, La Maison Douce was reworked under the innovative inspiration of a young couple eager to show off their sense of hospitality. With its floors inlaid with pebbles, white or caramel quilted bedspreads, butter-colored fabrics, armchairs covered in potato sacks, clocks made of bronze, and enameled bathtubs in delightfully old-fashioned bathrooms, the house and its alcoves thrive on the Isle de Ré spirit. And the bedrooms? They'll satisfy even the most die hard of romantics.

- 9 rooms: $90–$170.
- 2 suites: $175.
- Breakfast: $12.
- Open year round.

Charente

Le Château de Maumont

Claudine Joly and Philippe Poirier, 4, rue Aristide Briand, 16600 Magnac-sur-Touvre.
Tel: 011 33 5 45 90 81 10. Fax: 011 33 5 45 37 37 95. hiram.deco@wanadoo.fr

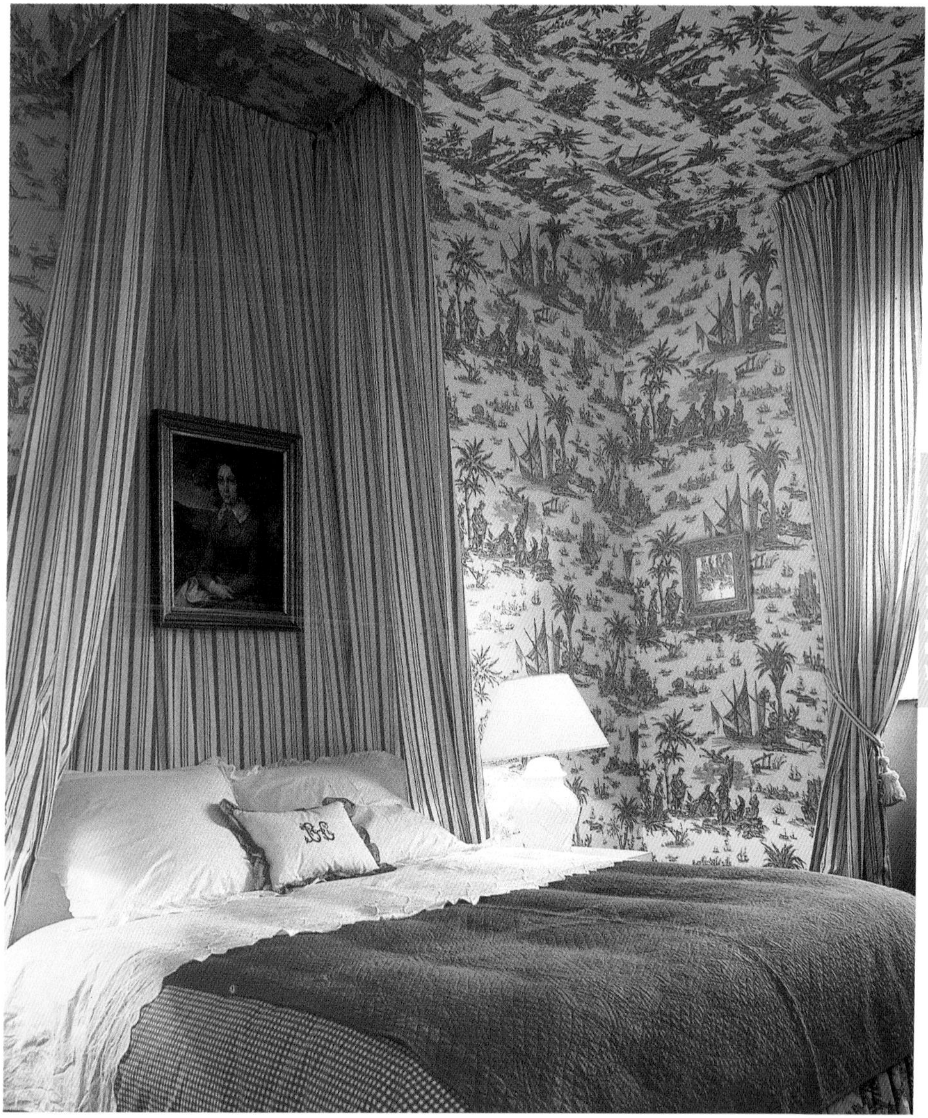

This Renaissance-era castle now enjoys a new life behind its façade of mullioned windows, covered in a voracious Virginia creeper. Surprisingly, what seduces here is the warmth. Goodbye to minimalism—owner Claudine Joly adores the drama of interior decor: a table standing in front of the fireplace; a candelabra with every candle lit; deep sofas with overlapping cushions. The grounds hide green spaces to be discovered on a beautiful day, such as the small courtyard in the back with its mossy stairs. Claudine is partial to the 18th century princess' rooms, decked in lace, little bottles, and china. If you appreciate this style of design, don't miss "La Chambre Rose" ("The Pink Bedroom"), which will seduce you with its raspberry fabrics and spring bouquets.

- 3 rooms: $100.
- 1 suite: $160.
- Breakfast included.
- Meals: $35.
- Open year round.

Le Logis du Portal

Mr. and Mrs. Berthommé, 16330 Vars.
Tel: 011 33 5 45 20 38 19. Fax: 011 33 5 45 68 94 24.

Set between two pillars elegantly joined by a basket-handle arch, a gate opens onto a courtyard shaded by big, centuries-old trees. All around it is a quadrangle of buildings made of golden stone. Enhanced by rose bushes, fruit trees, and a grapevine, and with the Charente river gurgling nearby, the Logis du Portal has a wonderful setting. Walls in hues of raspberry, saffron, and lemon-yellow complement the contemporary furniture of glass and wrought iron—which poses a contrast to the austerity of the Louis XIII furniture in the dining room. A staircase leads to romantic rooms in mauve Jouy fabrics, one Empire-style in green accents, a family atmosphere in powder blue for another.

- 3 rooms: $65.
- 1 suite: $100.
- Breakfast included.
- Pool.
- Open year round.

PARIS
VERSAILLES
ILE-DE-FRANCE
ARGENTAN
DREUX
RAMBOUILLET
EVRY
MELUN
PROVINS
VITRY-LE-FRANÇOIS
SAINT-DIZIER
BAR-LE-DUC
COMMERCY
ALENÇON
MORTAGNE-AU-PERCHE
Eure
Sarthe
CHARTRES
ETAMPES
FONTAINEBLEAU
NOGENT-SUR-SEINE
Seine
CHAMPAGNE-ARDENNE
Aube
NEUFCHATEAU
MAMERS
NOGENT-LE-ROTROU
TROYES
SENS
BAR-SUR-AUBE
CHAUMONT
PITHIVIERS
CHATEAUDUN
LE MANS
PAYS-DE-LA-LOIRE
ORLEANS
Chécy
MONTARGIS
AUXERRE
LANGRES
VENDOME
Ménestreau-en-Villette
LA FLECHE
BLOIS
Mont-près-Chambord
MONTBARD
Saône
AVALLON
Rochecorbon
CENTRE
CLAMECY
Chouzé-s-Loire
TOURS
Vouvray
Loire
ROMORANTIN-LANTHENAY
Cher
SAUMUR
Montigny
COSNE-COURS-SUR LOIRE
Yonne
BOURGOGNE
DIJON
CHINON
VIERZON
LOCHES
Bourges
Aloxe-Corton
Doubs
DOLE
Indre
CHATEAU-CHINON
AUTUN
BEAUNE
ISSOUDUN
NEVERS
CHATELLERAULT
SAINT-AMAND-MONTROND
CHALON-SUR-SAONE
LONS-LE-SAUNIER
CHATEAUROUX
Baudrières
LE BLANC
Orval
Creuse
POITIERS
LA CHATRE
MOULINS
LOUHANS
Ain
MONTMORILLON
CHAROLLES
MACON
BOURG-EN-BRESSE
MONTLUÇON
Allier
POITOU-CHARENTES
Vienne
GUERET
Vicq
VICHY
NANTUA
VILLEFRANCHE-SUR-SAONE
BELLAC
St-Hilaire-le-Château
ROANNE
AUBUSSON
AUVERGNE
CONFOLENS
St-Jean-St-Maurice
LIMOGES
St-Pardoux-le-Neuf
RIOM
THIERS
BELLE
ROCHECHOUART
CLERMONT-FERRAND
Aubusson-d'Auvergne
LYON
RHONE-ALPES
LIMOUSIN
MONTBRISON
Loire
ANGOULEME
Montaigut-le-Blanc
Chadeleuf
USSEL
ISSOIRE
AMBERT
VIENNE
LA TOUR-DU-PIN
NONTRON
SAINT-ETIENNE
TULLE
BRIOUDE
BRIVE-LA-GAILLARDE
MAURIAC
St-Arcons-d'Allier
YSSINGEAUX
PERIGUEUX
Beaulieu-s-Dordogne
SAINT-FLOUR
TOURNON
SARLAT-LA-CANEDA
AURILLAC
LE PUY-EN-VELAY
VALENCE
BERGERAC
0
50
100 km
DIE
GOURDON
PRIVAS

Centre-Auvergne

La Maison
19120 Beaulieu-sur-Dordogne.

Les Vergnes
23200 Saint-Pardoux-le-Neuf.

Château de la Chassagne
23250 Saint-Hilaire-le-Château.

Le Chastel Montaigu
63320 Montaigut-le-Blanc.

La Vigie
63320 Chadeleuf.

Le Moulin de Vernières
63120 Aubusson-d'Auvergne.

Les Deux Abbesses
43300 Saint-Arcons-d'Allier.

L'Echauguette
42155 Saint Jean-Saint-Maurice-sur-Loire.

La Chaumière
71370 Baudrières.

La Villa Louise
21420 Aloxe-Corton.

Le Manoir de La Mothe
03450 Vicq.

La Reculée en Berry
18250 Montigny.

Le Domaine de la Trolière
18200 Orval.

Les Bonnets Rouges
18000 Bourges.

Le Château des Réaux
37140 Chouzé-sur-Loire.

Le Domaine des Bidaudières
37210 Vouvray.

Le Château de Montgouverne
37210 Rochecorbon.

Le Manoir de Clénord
41250 Mont-près-Chambord.

Les Courtils
45430 Chécy.

La Ferme des Foucault
45240 Ménestreau-en-Villette.

La Maison

11, rue de la Gendarmerie, 19120 Beaulieu-sur-Dordogne.
Tel: 011 33 5 55 91 24 97. Fax: 011 33 5 55 91 51 27.

La Maison opens onto a patio decorated with hydrangeas and lemon trees. Guests meet for breakfast under the ancient coach house, or, in the evenings, for *apéritifs* around a bar covered in bright mosaics. On the other side of the courtyard, the bedrooms are a mix of styles and ambiences: Some are Provençal —mainly red with inlaid cobbled floors; others are more natural in gray and yellow, with bedcovers printed with Far-West motifs. In the main part of the house, there's a comfy purple room, another with objects found in a flea market, and a bride's bedroom that splices white muslin with a fabric as blue as the southern seas atop a canopy bed made of planks.

- 6 rooms: $50–$65.
- Breakfast included.
- Pool.
- Closed from October 1 to March 31.

Les Vergnes

Creuse

Mr. and Mrs. Dumontant, 23200 Saint-Pardoux-le-Neuf. **Tel: 011 33 5 55 66 23 74.**
Fax: 011 33 5 55 67 74 16. sylvie.dumontant@freesbee.fr

Les Vergnes is a 17th century former farmer's house with six guest rooms, each done up to express a different kind of journey. The most exotic is "Retour des Indes" ("Return to the Indies"), with an elephant motif printed on the hem of plum-colored drapes. The dark brown furniture fits in perfectly with the straw-colored carpets, and the bathrooms made of old marble are magnificent. With its patchwork of colored squares, "Miró" is the obvious name for one room hung with honey-colored drapes and wall coverings, and filled with English furniture. It's a more traditional ambience for "Provence," with its filtered lighting coming from a pretty lampshade made by innkeeper Sylvie Dumontant, who is also known to delight her guests' palates with her regional specialties.

- 6 rooms: $45–$75.
- 1 suite: $90.
- Meals: $20.
- Pool.
- Open year round.

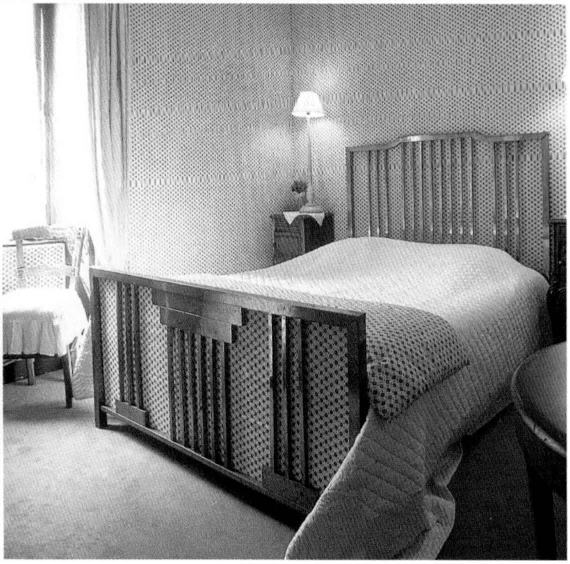

Château de la Chassagne

Mr. and Mrs. Fanton, 23250 Saint-Hilaire-le-Château.
Tel: 011 33 5 55 64 55 75. Fax: 011 33 5 55 64 90 92.

This beautiful fortress established in a wooded grove dates from the 15th century. After having belonged to the Aubusson family, it was transformed into a country hospital during the war. It was restored thanks to the dedication and passion of two hoteliers from the neighboring village, so today its role has changed from one of defense to one of pleasure. The rooms, with their medieval frames but modern comforts, are distributed around a granite spiral staircase. The largest, entirely covered by woodwork matching an antique canopy bed, is accompanied by a huge bathroom with a Jacuzzi. One room is decked in pink toile de Jouy that shows the old chestnut floor. The same treatment for its neighbor, draped in slate-gray Jouy fabric and with twin Empire beds. A more bourgeois bedroom opens to views of the park. And in the morning, look forward to breakfast in the Louis XIII dining room, in front of the chimney with its blazing log fire.

- Rooms: $70–$95.
- Breakfast included.
- Open year round.

Le Chastel Montaigu

63320 Montaigut-le-Blanc.
Tel: 011 33 4 73 96 28 49. Fax: 011 33 4 73 96 21 60.

A building contractor and his wife threw themselves into the Herculean task of raising this castle from ruins. The outcome: In the morning, you breakfast in a 12th century dining room, having had a good night's sleep under the canopy of the "Gothic room." But the owners have taken care to balance history and modernity: Behind exposed timbers and pink brick walls, a bathroom has been equipped with creature comforts. During another stay, try the "Chambre du Ravin" ("The Ravine Room"), with contemporary flooring stenciled with foliage. Its panoramic bathroom gives you an overhead view of Rodde valley, and come springtime, watch for the peregrine falcons that come to nest in the recess of its window. They say it's a sign of good luck.

- 5 rooms: $90–$125.
- Breakfast included.
- Closed last week of June, Christmas week, January, and February.

La Vigie

Mr. and Mrs. Pineau, 3, rue de la Muscadière, 63320 Chadeleuf.
Tel: 011 33 4 73 96 90 87. Fax: 011 33 4 73 96 92 76. pineau.denis@wanadoo.fr

The house hadn't been lived in for 50 years, then one day, it woke up to a cascade of children's laughter, brought on by the arrival of the young couple who have taken up the task of restoring this guest house. The family ambience can be sensed in the decor of the two guest bedrooms. In "Ivoire" hang full linen drapes, held by knotted raffia. Beams of powdered white brighten up family furniture in this big room with a chimney made of granite from Montpeyroux. You'll find the same embroidered linen in the "Blue" room, imbued with romanticism with its frieze of wisterias. The house has a Bohemian mood, from the garden where you can linger on summer evenings to the very comfortable lounge, where you can snuggle up and watch the logs crackle in the hearth.

- 2 rooms: $55–$65.
- Breakfast included.
- Meals: $20.
- Pool.
- Closed for Christmas.

Le Moulin des Vernières

Mrs. Hansen, 63120 Aubusson-d'Auvergne.
Tel/fax: 011 33 4 73 53 53 01. www.moulindesvernieres.com

Spring brings it to life: The small house with slate blue shutters, drowned under roses and jasmine, has its garden rooms in a decor a little mad but disciplined by a gifted innkeeper who also happens to be quite a cook. There may be pink trout on a bed of lentils and garlic for dinner; tomorrow perhaps a potato and cheese truffade. At Suzette Hansen's, you really feel like you're staying with a friend. Acquaintances are made in the big lounge-cum-library, artistic ideas are exchanged in front of photographs by Doisneau. The small rustic rooms, inspired by grandmother's furniture, are truly intimate. And it's in the old stable, illuminated by an immense glass roof, that people come together for a drink. From there, the views of the meadows are yours for the taking.

- 3 rooms: $60.
- 1 suite: $70.
- Breakfast included.
- Meals: $20.
- Closed from November 16 to February 15.

Les Deux Abbesses

Laurence Perceval-Hermet, Le Château, 43300 Saint-Arcons-d'Allier.
Tel: 011 33 4 71 74 03 08. Fax: 011 33 4 71 74 05 30.
www.les-deux-abbesses.fr direction@les-deux-abbesses.fr

With its entrance in a pretty, 12th century mansion transformed during the Renaissance by the two abbesses who gave it its name, Deux Abbesses offers 10 rooms lorded over by innkeeper Laurence Perceval-Hermet. For twenty years, she led a fast-paced career in New York and Tokyo. Today, she's put down anchor at the confluence of the Allier and Fioule rivers. And the rooms at Deux Abbesses: regional furniture with box beds and canopies, quilts or white comforters, carpets, selected ornaments, and works by contemporary artists.

- 11 rooms: $100–$250.
- Breakfast: $17.
- Meals: $45.
- Pool.
- Closed from November 12 to April 20.

L'Echauguette

Mr. and Mrs. Alex, ruelle Guy-de-la-Mûre, 42155 Saint-Jean-Saint-Maurice-sur-Loire.
Tel: 011 33 4 77 63 15 89.

It's hard to imagine today that, in an extraordinary setting of savage gorges, this used to be one of the most difficult passages of the Loire's course. But almost 20 years ago, a dam and lake were constructed to control the rising water level. Now, L'Echauguette enjoys the wonderful setting. Preceded by a small lounge, the first guest room offers a view of the now-calm waters. In a former tearoom, a second bedroom uses tones of soft yellow and almond green, while the one on the first floor has a powdery whiteness spiced with red, and offers a view onto the 12th century church in the medieval town below.

- 4 rooms: $45–$65.
- Breakfast included.
- Menus: $20.
- Open year round.

La Chaumière

Arlette Vachet, route de Saint-Germain-du-Plain, 71370 Baudrières.
Tel: 011 33 3 85 47 32 18. Fax: 011 33 3 85 47 41 42. Cell: 011 33 6 07 49 53 46.

Under a roof of flat tiles, chiseled beams support rooms warmed by a fire. The lounge, with its timbered niches, collected trinkets, and flowery cloths, welcomes guests to stay a while. A shell collection sits alongside armchairs perked up with madras cotton. With its regional furniture given a lift with finds brought back from long journeys, owner Arlette Vachet's home is truly unique. The bedrooms play in this same vein, flowery and offbeat, in hues of red cherry, yellow, and turquoise.

- 2 rooms: $60.
- 1 suite: $70.
- Breakfast included.
- Pool.
- Closed from Halloween to Easter.

La Villa Louise

Véronique Perrin, 9, rue Franche. 21420 Aloxe-Corton. **Tel: 011 33 3 80 26 46 70.**
Fax: 011 33 3 80 26 47 16. www.hotel-villa-louise.fr hotel-villa-louise@wanadoo.fr

Say the Côte-d'Or, and a string of charming places come to mind, such as Aloxe-Corton, a typical small Burgundy village with its roofs of glazed tiles. Véronique Perrin—third generation of winemakers—welcomes guests to the Villa Louise, a beautiful 17th century building. The vineyard, its cellars, and the bedrooms are all done in a warm decor—both cozy and elegant. The red brick, nougat, and pink quilting with an accent of raspberry or yellow are a perfect match for the brown beams, the chocolate, white, or dark brown armchairs, and the bathroom basins in pinkish beige stone. The scene is set to enjoy a fire in the lounge, from which you can watch the day come to a close while relaxing into a comfy club armchair.

- 10 rooms: $75–$150.
- Breakfast: $12.
- Open year round.

Allier

Le Manoir de La Mothe

Mr. and Mrs. Van Merris, 03450 Vicq.
Tel: 011 33 4 70 58 51 90. Fax: 011 33 4 70 58 52 02. MichelvanMerris@aol.com

It's a real fairy tale castle surrounded by moats, filled with swans and ducks. To enter, you go over a drawbridge—the same kind as in medieval times—restored about 10 years ago by a Flemish couple who had fallen under the spell of the place.

- 2 rooms: $90–$95.
- 1 cottage with 3 rooms: $400–$600 for a week.
- Breakfast included.
- Meals: $35.
- Pool.
- Open year round.

The decor in the bedrooms and suites respects the spirit of the chateau while adding splashes of color, such as a bathroom bordered by blue shellfish in the "Boulangerie," suite. A soft copper glow in the suite "de la Tour," papered with stripes and dusty pink flowers. An original chimney warms the mezzanine. In the main part of the building, you come across another room, "des Gardes," done in bluish pastels. The "du Château" room is marked by superb twisting floor tiles. And all around, good scents pervade: fresh wax mingling with the aroma of apples cooking in the oven in the chateau's kitchen.

La Reculée en Berry

Cher

Elisabeth Gressin, 18250 Montigny.
Tel: 011 33 2 48 69 59 18. Fax: 011 33 2 48 69 52 51. e.gressin@terre-net.fr

This beautiful house with Virginia creeper clinging to the façade sits in the foothills of Sancerre. Five guest rooms have been installed here in the old stables. "Liseron" is decked in pink and blue. "Bleuet" bathes in the morning sun. The colors in "Bouton d'or" are tones found in exotic fruits. There is also "Primevère," with a grandmother's copper bed. But most beautiful is "Coquelicot": A bouquet of red flowers placed on a simple country table works so well with the big red-checkered spread that covers the bed. And because a swallow built its nest behind the skylight on the eve of a wedding night, innkeeper Elisabeth Gressin always reserves it for lovers.

- 5 rooms: $50.
- Breakfast included.
- Meals: $20.
- Closed from November 15 to March 15.

Le Domaine de la Trolière

Marie-Claude Dussert, 18200 Orval.
Tel: 011 33 2 48 96 47 45. Fax: 011 33 2 48 96 07 71.

A mossy path opens up onto a beautiful 18th century home hidden behind leaves. Marie-Claude Dussert is absolutely mad about toile de Jouy—it can be seen in every color in her house, starting with the lounge, where the hue of the old paving stones gave her the idea to cover the seats in blue Jouy. The dining room, where delicious breakfasts are served, is decorated in yellow and gray Jouy fabrics. On the second floor, three rooms opt for romanticism with grayish-blue and autumn hues. "Jaune"—the "Yellow" room—is the one place where Jouy fabrics aren't used. Instead, there are stripes bordered by an English frieze of rosebuds. There's an en suite bathroom for one room, and a shared one on the landing for the other two.

- 3 rooms: $50–$60.
- 1 cottage, sleeps 5/6: $320–$375 for a week, $200 for a weekend (2 nights minimum).
- Breakfast included.
- Meals: $20.
- Open year round.

Les Bonnets Rouges

Nathalie and Olivier Llopis, 3, rue de la Thaumassière, 18000 Bourges. **Tel: 011 33 2 48 65 79 92.**
Fax: 011 33 2 48 69 82 05. http://bonnets-rouges.bourges.net bonnets-rouges@bourges.net

At the bend in a paved street in old Bourges, a *Phrygian* cap—liberty cap—used as a sign, catches your attention. It turns out that the building already existed as a hotel in the 15th century, under the name of "Boeuf Couronné." Stendhal spoke about it, Mérimée stayed there. When the former owners bought the house, they didn't know about all the treasures behind its ruined walls. In the end, under all that cracked plaster, they discovered superb woodwork and stone walls that had survived the centuries. Today, Nathalie and Olivier Llopis have taken over the reins of the house and continue to serve breakfasts in a dining room with exposed stone walls, its tables covered in tablecloths with romantic motifs. Homemade cakes and yogurts, and bowls of fruit in a setting filled with second-hand goods are just part of early mornings here.

- 2 rooms: $60–$70.
- 2 suites: $65–$80.
- Breakfast included.
- Open year round.

Le Château des Réaux

Mr. and Mrs. Goupil de Bouillé, Le Port-Boulet, 37140 Chouzé-sur-Loire. **Tel: 011 33 2 47 95 14 40.**
Fax: 011 33 2 47 95 18 34. www.chateaux-france.com/-reaux reaux@chateaux-france.com

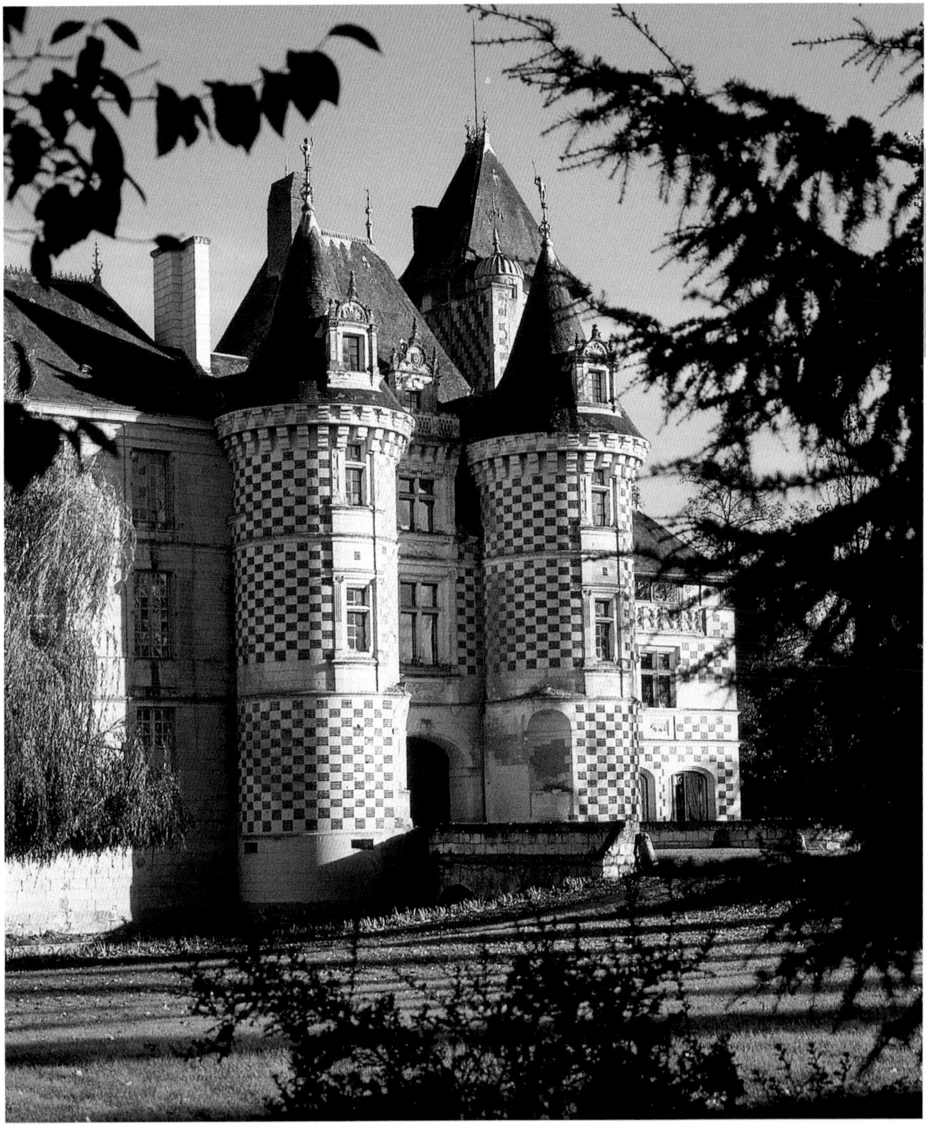

When it comes to making guests feel welcome in a chateau, Florence Goupil de Bouillé is a pioneer. After 25 years of mastering her art, she has become a reference point—ever since the day in 1976 when her husband decided to purchase the castle of their ancestors and open it up to tourists in need of hospitality. Little by little, the rooms have nibbled away all the spaces of this pretty mansion with a pink and white brick checkerboard façade. And Florence continues to delight guests with her infectious zest for life, taking them around to visit every castle in the Valley of the Kings before tucking them in to one of her 16 alcoves, each loaded with history. The newest room, called "le Bas de la tour," is done in shades of green and pink on a background of brick. The large contemporary carpet that warms the lounge signals the new spirit of the place. The other rooms play upon the romanticism of the Touraine. Also, a cottage offers those with smaller budgets a way to treat themselves for as little as $100 a night.

- 17 rooms and suites: $130–$230.
- Breakfast: $15.
- Meals: $50.
- Closed for Christmas.

Le Domaine des Bidaudières

Mr. and Mrs. Suzanne, rue du Peu-Morier, 37210 Vouvray. **Tel: 011 33 2 47 52 66 85.**
Fax: 011 33 2 47 52 62 17. www.bidaudieres.com info@bandb-loire-valley.com

The young couple who own this castle, built on a 17th century winegrowing domain, added adjoining troglodytic cellars—an act that speaks to their contemporary vision. The shell of the building remains classic but the inside has been entirely rethought for the 21st century. The old partitions were demolished to create well-lit spaces, and a huge elevator has been installed to serve rooms swathed in some of the most beautiful fabric designs. The rooms may have taken their names from Touraine vineyards, but their aesthetic leans unquestionably toward contemporary Italian design. Flaxen marquetries, large floral prints, stylized leafage, and pink ginghams hallmark the look of the alcoves. On the ground floor, a long succession of reception rooms survey a landscape of cascading terraces and vineyards that vanish over the swimming pool, replaced with views of the Loire and its confluent, the Cisse.

- 5 rooms: $110.
- 1 suite: $125.
- Breakfast included.
- Pool.
- Open year round.

Le Château de Montgouverne

Laurent and Nicola Gross, 37210 Rochecorbon. **Tel: 011 33 2 47 52 84 59.**
Fax: 011 33 2 47 52 84 61. www.montgouverne.com info@montgouverne.com

The sophistication of this property's ancient enclosed garden will seduce you right away, but the romantic atmosphere of this chateau is everywhere—from the lounges to the bedrooms, and not even forgetting the bathrooms. From one room, "Heure Bleue," done in cornflower hues, to another, "Lilas," in shades of mauve and red berries, the decor delights the senses. In "Petit Matin," it is from under a trellised grapevine that you'll watch the sun rise. And "Volets Clos" offers a country ambience which suits the Touraine as much as it does the chateau.

- 4 rooms: $100-$140.
- 2 suites: $140–$170.
- Breakfast: $10.
- Meals: $40.
- Pool.
- Open year round.
- No pets allowed.

Le Manoir de Clénord

998, route de Clénord, 41250 Mont-près-Chambord. **Tel: 011 33 2 54 70 41 62.**
Fax: 011 33 2 54 70 33 99. www.clenord.com info@clenord.com

On its courtyard side, Clénord reveals a bourgeois residence draped with Virginia creeper and covered by slates. On the garden side, barns the color of burnt bread, and a freshly cut lawn reveal a slightly Tuscan air. Around the swimming pool, heather gives way, in summer, to a few patches of lavender framed by cypress trees. The place is elegant, hushed. Its origins go back to the 15th century, but the following centuries also brought a succession of changes to flood every room with light. Six guest rooms, of which three are suites, have been appointed with English fabrics in harmony with the colors of the Sologne. Sea-green and Loire blue are the dominant colors. With two or three details that make all the difference, such as bound books set on a nightstand, or bathroom tiling coordinated to match the colors of the bedroom, elegance is the theme of the day.

- 5 rooms and 3 suites: $70–$200.
- Breakfast included.
- Pool, tennis.
- Closed from November 15 to March 31.

Les Courtils

Annie Meunier, rue de l'Avé, 45430 Chécy.
Tel: 011 33 2 38 91 32 02. Fax: 011 33 2 38 91 48 20.

This pretty house, nestled at the foot of a church, was restored by Annie Meunier in a very personal style that transcends time. Variations in beige and off-white for the lounge, and bedrooms that borrow their names from the flowers in the garden. There's "Volubilis," with its array of plant illustrations and its view of the Loire in the background; "Chèvrefeuille," with its delicate portraits by François Legrand, a local artist, whose prints in blue-grey lend a soft tone to the room. Unabashedly more colorful, "Coloquinte" and "Capucines" throw a ray of light into the house with their Deco atmospheres. In every bathroom, a stenciled frieze enhances mirrors and walls, and from the big terrace, you can see from the Gâtinais plain all the way to the horizons that vanish into the Loire itself.

- 4 rooms: $50.
- Breakfast included.
- Open year round.

La Ferme des Foucault

Loiret

Rosemary Beau, 45240 Ménestreau-en-Villette.
Tel/fax: 011 33 2 38 76 94 41. rbeau@waika9.com

Right in the thick of Sologne, on the land of a former agricultural domain, sits this small farm and its barns. The new owners had the wisdom to leave its courtyard fallow and the foresight to open the interior timbers to let in lots of light. A golden mirror hangs over the white lounge in which a red sofa sits. It's an atmosphere of quietude against a light background and stripped beams. The rooms and the suite are immense and luminous. Large or irregular, there are three or four windows per room. Innkeeper Rosemary Beau, originally from Boston, has retained the sense of space and the taste for the cozy, homey interiors of the East Coast, mingled with the materials of Sologne. A bit of Indonesian furniture here, a flowery tablecloth there, all help to get the point across.

- 2 rooms and 1 suite: $65–$75.
- Breakfast included.
- Open year round.

NORD-PAS-DE-CALAIS
DUNKERQUE
CALAIS
BOULOGNE-SUR-MER
SAINT-OMER
LILLE
Sailly-s-la-Lys
Montreuil-s-Mer
BETHUNE
LENS
DOUAI
VALENCIENNES
ARRAS
CAMBRAI
AVESNES-SUR-HELPE
PICARDIE
St-Valéry-s-Somme
DIEPPE
HAUTE-NORMANDIE
LE HAVRE
ROUEN
Risle
LES ANDELYS
Vironvay
Giverny
Seine
BERNAY
EVREUX
MANTES-LA-JOLIE
CHERBOURG
BAYEUX
CAEN
LISIEUX
SAINT-LO
Notre-Dame-de-Livaye
Les Moutiers-Hubert
COUTANCES
BASSE-NORMANDIE
VIRE
AVRANCHES
ARGENTAN
DREUX
MORTAGNE-AU-PERCHE
Eure
CHARTRES
ALENÇON
Sarthe
Saint-Paterne
MAMERS
NOGENT-LE-ROTROU
Plouguiel
St-Méloir-des-Ondes
LANNION
SAINT-MALO
Plélo
MORLAIX
GUINGAMP
BREST
Le Conquet
Plougonven
SAINT-BRIEUC
DINAN
Bazouges-la-Pérouse
Rance
Aulne
CHATEAULIN
FOUGERES
Bécherel
Landudec
QUIMPER
Ste-Marine
BRETAGNE
PONTIVY
Rennes
MAYENNE
Mayenne
Rouez-en-Champagne
CHATEAUDUN
LAVAL
LE MANS
LORIENT
VANNES
Asnières-s-Vègre
CHATEAU-GONTIER
VENDOME
REDON
Vilaine
CHATEAUBRIANT
LA FLECHE
SEGRE
Briollay
BLOIS
ANGERS
ANCENIS
PAYS-DE-LA-LOIRE
TOURS
CENTRE
SAINT-NAZAIRE
Loire
SAUMUR
ROMORANTIN-LANTHENAY
NANTES
Fontevraud-l'Abbaye
CHINON
CHOLET
LOCHES
Indre
BRESSUIRE
CHATELLERAULT
CHATEAUROUX
LA ROCHE-SUR-YON
Angles-s-l'Anglin
LES SABLES-D'OLONNE
Mervent
PARTHENAY
LE BLANC
Creuse
POITIERS
FONTENAY-LE-COMTE
NIORT
MONTMORILLON
LA ROCHELLE
Vienne
0
50
100 km
POITOU-CHARENTES
BELLAC
ROCHEFORT
SAINT-JEAN-D'ANGELY
CONFOLENS
LIMOGES
SAINTES
ROCHECHOUART

West and North

Le Lyon d'Or
86260 Angles-sur-l'Anglin.

Le Logis de la Cornelière
85200 Mervent.

Le Château de Noirieux
49125 Briollay.

Le Domaine de Mestre
49590 Fontevraud-l'Abbaye.

L'Abbaye de Champagne
72140 Rouez-en-Champagne.

Le Château de Saint-Paterne
72610 Saint-Paterne.

La Seigneurie des Claies
72430 Asnières-sur-Vègre.

La Filanderie
35190 Bécherel.

Lecoq-Gadby
35700 Rennes.

Le Château de la Ballue
35560 Bazouges-la-Pérouse.

Le Château Richeux
35350 Saint-Méloir-des-Ondes.

L'Hôtel Sainte-Marine
29120 Sainte-Marine.

Le Château de Guilguiffin
29710 Landudec.

Le Relais du Vieux Port
29217 Le Conquet.

La Grange de Coatelan
29640 Plougonven.

Le Château de Lezhildry
22220 Plouguiel.

Le Char à bancs
22170 Plélo.

Le Domaine de Clairvaux
14140 Les Moutiers-Hubert.

Les Pommiers de Livaye
14340 Notre-Dame-de-Livaye.

La Réserve
27620 Giverny.

Les Saisons
27400 Vironvay.

La Gribane
80230 Saint-Valéry-sur-Somme.

L'Auberge de la Grenouillère
62170 Montreuil-sur-Mer.

Station Bac Saint-Maur
62840 Sailly-sur-la-Lys.

Le Lyon d'Or

Mr. and Mrs. Thoreau, Route de Vicq, 86260 Angles-sur-l'Anglin. **Tel: 011 33 5 49 48 32 53.**
Fax: 011 33 5 49 84 02 28. www.lyondor.com thoreau@lyondor.com

Situated in a village that's been rated among the "Plus Beaux de France"— Most Beautiful Villages of France—Lyon d'Or offered a second life for owner Guillaume Thoreau. The former London banker left the banks of the Thames, bringing with him his young English wife, for a dwelling steeped in history. The walls had not had a sweeping since the 14th century. Today, they've been restored by local artisans and by Heather Thoreau, who has painted them in ochre and soft blues. She has stenciled ivy leaves onto them and veiled the imitation canopy beds with muslin covered with patchwork, and given a sheen to the walls and furniture according to old techniques which she reveals to visitors on her "Special Interior Decoration" weekends. All in all, the Lyon d'Or has become one of those delightful little country hotels where, in the evenings, guests show off their rooms to one another. As for the food, the Thoreaus sit proudly at the head of one of the best tables in the region.

- 10 rooms: $60–$100.
- Breakfast: $10.
- Half-board: $55–$70.
- Closed in January and February.

Le Logis de la Cornelière

Jean-Raymond and Lyse de Larocque Latour, 85200 Mervent. **Tel: 011 33 2 51 00 29 25.**
www.corneliere.com corneliere.mervent@libertysurf.fr

With its enclosed courtyard typical of the architecture in the Vendée, this house was originally fortified and surrounded by a moat. Warm, ochre-colored stones discovered among the rubble have helped restore its original grandeur. The fireplace in the living room was also uncovered during the rebuilding, as was the staircase that leads to the "Bleue" ("Blue") bedroom, which is huge and nostalgic in style. The Henry II beds were snatched from as far afield as Switzerland and covered with a damask for the "Verte" ("Green") suite. Dusty-pink limewash coats a third bedroom which opens out onto the courtyard. The inn has been installed in an old chapel, whose small arched windows have been preserved. Then there's the "Jaune" ("Yellow") bedroom, set up in the old stables, where the pride of the room is a beautiful 18th century bed. In the evenings, guests gather in the dining room around the 16th century fireplace found on the property while it was being used as steps for building a wall.

- 3 rooms: $85.
- 1 suite: $110.
- Breakfast: $10.
- Pool.
- Gym.
- Open year round.

Le Château de Noirieux

Mr. and Mrs. Come, 26, route du Moulin, 49125 Briollay.
Tel: 011 33 2 41 42 50 05. Fax: 011 33 2 41 37 91 00.

The soft light of spring, the pastel skies, the pure air—all of this inspires walks or morning jogs on the paths around this inn that wind down towards the Loire. Noirieux is far more of a country castle than it appears at first sight. The morning sun hits the stone of the classical façade erected under Louis XIV. The light plays with the hangings on the drawing room walls and bathes the golden wood in sunshine. An Art Deco spiral staircase made of stone polished like ivory unwinds right up to the bedrooms, whose style vary between contemporary and romantic. The "Art Deco" bedroom is accompanied by a magnificent bathroom with an old-style mosaic. Other rooms sport a more country vibe, and are located in the outbuildings of the domain (which most likely owes its name to the walnuts that were cultivated there).

- 18 rooms: $160–$300.
- Breakfast: $20.
- Meals: $45–$85.
- Closed from February 6 to March 8, and from October 27 to November 21.

Le Domaine de Mestre

Rosine Dauge, 49590 Fontevraud-l'Abbaye. **Tel: 011 33 2 41 51 75 87.**
Fax: 011 33 2 41 51 71 90. www.dauge-fontevraud.com domaine-de-mestre@wanadoo.fr

This 12th century farm overflows with a country ambience so particular to the banks of the Loire River. Innkeeper Rosine Dauge and her daughters were so won over by English Country interior design that they've decorated every room in romantic materials and wallpapers—from the drapes to the friezes. Each room has, nevertheless, its own personal style: a grape motif and a pitch pine bed for one, Art Deco furniture for another. In all the other rooms they've used country and ancestral furniture, such as a desk straight out of a Balzac novel that occupies one alcove. Ivy patterns, copper chandeliers, and bathroom linens complementing the colors of the rooms all emphasize the country spirit of these spaces. Rosine Dauge also makes scented soaps that are distributed worldwide. They are developed in her workshop, situated in the old barn beneath a room that used to serve as a shelter for pilgrims on their way to Santiago de Compostela.

- 12 rooms and suites: $40–$100.
- Breakfast: $7.
- Dinner: $25.
- Closed from December 20 to March 1.

Sarthe

L'Abbaye de Champagne

Mrs. Luzu, 72140 Rouez-en-Champagne. **Tel: 011 33 2 43 20 15 74. Fax: 011 33 2 43 20 74 61.**
www.abbayedechampagne.com contact@abbayedecahmapgne.com

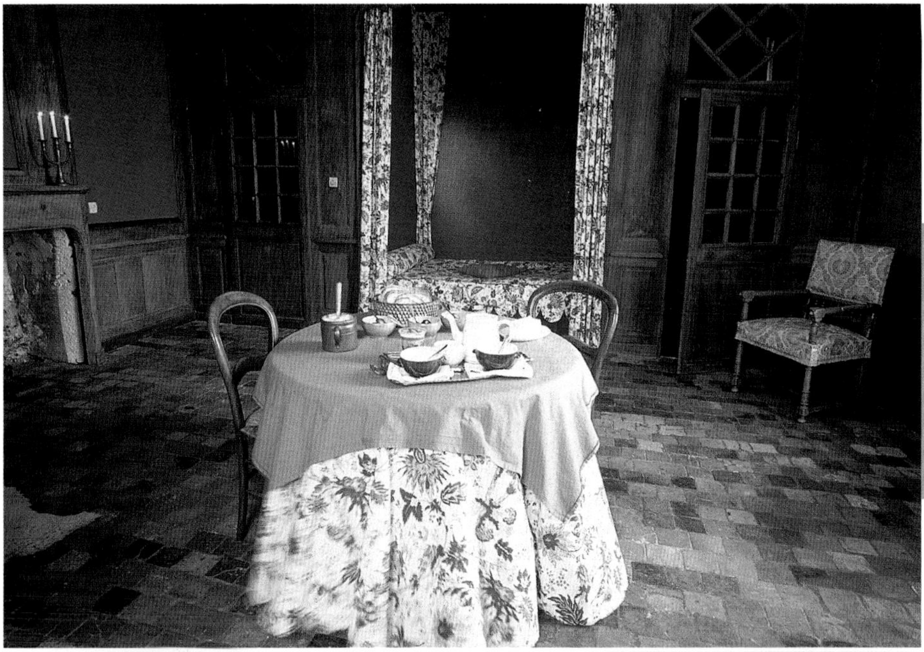

Renovated at the beginning of the 20th century by a farming family determined to give it back its soul, this Cistercian Abbey is nothing short of a nature retreat. The old monk's shop has become a dining room serving real country cooking. The wine cellar, where fragments of 18th century frescoes remain, is now the reception area. And then there are the three bedrooms, aptly named: "Ficelle" ("String"), "Blé" ("Wheat"), and "Avoine" ("Oats"), all converted in the attic. "Avoine" is magnificent with its paneling surrounding a 17th century fireplace. Dusty pink tones for "Blé," almond green for "Ficelle." Throughout you'll find rustic tiles underfoot, heavy drapes, and interior wooden shutters. Amateur fly fishermen will enjoy the two lakes on the property, and a swimming pool has just opened near the orchard.

- 3 rooms: $50–$70.
- Breakfast included.
- Menus: $15–$25.
- Pool.
- Closed in February.

Le Château de Saint Paterne

Sarthe

Mr. and Mrs. de Valbray, 72610 Saint-Paterne. **Tel: 011 33 2 33 27 54 71.**
Fax: 011 33 2 33 29 16 71. www.chateau-saintpaterne.com paterne@club-internet.fr

The history of Saint Paterne was lost somewhere in the 15th century, but it's said that Henry IV, en route to the Battle of Ivry, spent a night here—and seduced the mistress of the house in the process. The golden initials of the King, intertwined with the initials of that mistress, Diane de Courtemanche, found on the woodwork of one of the rooms, may show proof of that night... Today, Charles-Henri and Ségolène de Valbray have breathed fresh air into the place by combining Eastern influences with touches of wit. An example is in the "A la Bastille" room, with its somber colors schemes sharing space with old, Indian rice scales and small confessional-style cloths. But the prettiest of all is the last room on a mezzanine in the attic honoring the new Lady of Saint Paterne with a small statue festooned with violet ribbons.

- 8 rooms and suites: $85–$200.
- Breakfast: $10.
- Dinner: $40.
- Pool.
- Closed from January 15 to April 1.

Sarthe

La Seigneurie des Claies

Mr. Anneron, Manoir lieu-dit des Claies, 72430 Asnières-sur-Vègre.
Tel: 011 33 2 43 92 40 50. Fax: 011 33 2 43 92 65 72.

A purple wisteria runs along the façade to the high, narrow windows that are typical of 15th century manor houses. An impressive stone staircase climbs the tower formerly reserved for nobles. Today, crowned with elm paneling, it leads to two bedrooms decorated in a red toile de Jouy with big, blue flowers. The owners of the manor have brightened it up without compromising its original character. Stone walls, floors covered in old-style tiles, all in natural sand-color for the most part, but draperies in vivid colors to reinject vitality into the interior. The suite on the garden level opens onto the meadows. There is a swimming pool in the garden, and the seasonal cuisine offered here is both fresh and inventive.

- 2 rooms and 1 suite: starting at $70.
- Breakfast included.
- Meals: $25.
- Pool.
- Closed from Halloween to Easter.

La Filanderie

Ille-et-Vilaine

Mr. and Mrs. Lecourtois-Canet, 3, rue de la Filanderie, 35190 Bécherel. **Tel: 011 33 2 99 66 73 17.**
Fax: 011 33 2 99 66 79 07. www.filanderie.com filanderie@aol.com

The owner of this property uses simple language to express her feelings about Brittany in general, but in particular about her home. It must be said that, with its half-timbering and painted blue woodwork, this place easily seduces passers-by. The tone is set, right away, in the kitchen, which is warm and friendly. The dining room opens onto creamy blues. This country atmosphere is extended to the garden, just as romantic as the bedrooms and hidden behind 15th century granite walls. The rooms, in their decor inspired by either historical or literary heroines, are decked in flowers, trellises, lace, knotted eiderdowns, and furniture with a hint of nostalgia. And, everywhere, leather-bound books are found on chests of drawers, bedside tables, or chairs with straw seats.

- 3 rooms: $45–$65.
- Additional bed: $17.
- Breakfast included.
- Closed from Easter to Halloween.

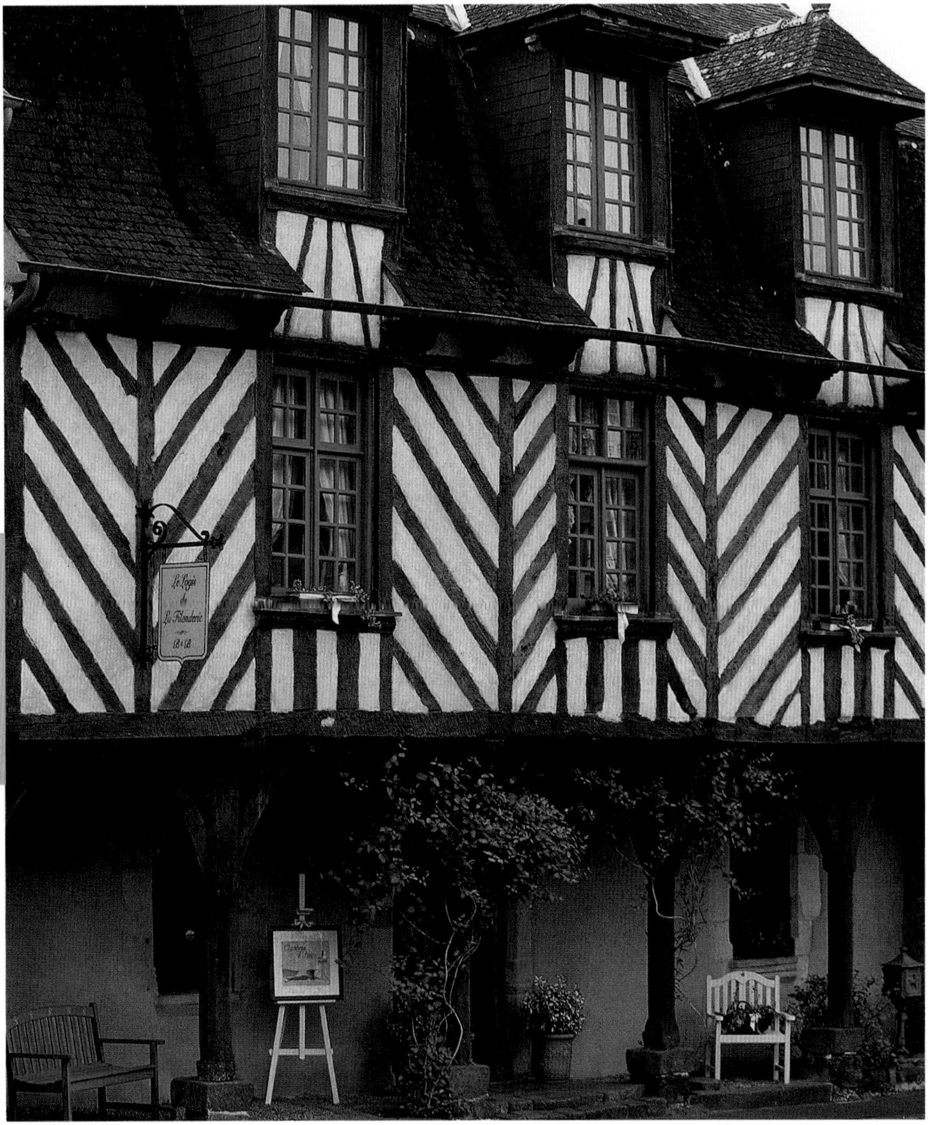

Lecoq-Gadby

156, rue d'Antrain, 35700 Rennes.
Tel: 011 33 2 99 38 05 55. Fax: 011 33 2 99 38 53 40.

There's the friendly and colorful reception lounge—creamy whites, dark reds, and ruby; and there's the farmyard, with a different feel altogether. Straw cockerels, collage cockerels, papier mâché cockerels, ceramic cockerels—the obvious mascot of Lecoq—are incorporated into the decor of this country inn. In the cozy atmosphere of a family home that combines flowers, fruit, stripes, ginghams,and Jouy prints there's a sense of well-being and plenty. It continues, on a more rustic note, in the dining room, where farm breakfasts are set up facing the garden and its leafy archways.
The bedrooms bring out this same spirit of elegance. Some more spacious that others, each room is individualized by the choice of fabrics used—all contemporary and of high quality. The cuisine, true to both the changing seasons and to Brittany, exemplifies the art of living well in this beautiful hotel.

- 10 rooms and 1 suite: $125–$150.
- Breakfast: starting at $15.
- Menus: $30–$60.
- Spa.
- Open year round.

Château de la Ballue

Château de la Ballue, 35560 Bazouges-la-Pérouse. **Tel: 011 33 2 99 97 47 86. Fax: 011 33 2 99 97 47 70.** www.laballue.com chateau@la-ballue.com

People come here for the gardens, but always get caught up in the magic of the whole place, including its rooms, inspired by history and literature. The chateau occupies a setting at once rustic, artistic, and intellectual. Its drawing rooms are a delicate blend of Asian ambiences with Breton atmospheres—wine-pickers' baskets and priceless paintings, batiks and granites. In the bedrooms, with shades of off-white, cream, and bright red, there's the same geography of blurred borders between one Persian alcove and another Florentine; between a French suite and immaculate woodwork. The bathrooms are underneath gazebos with irresistible little goodies scattered on courtesy trays.

- 5 rooms and 1 suite: starting at $150.
- Breakfast: $12.
- Jacuzzi, sauna.
- Closed from January 5 to February 16.

Le Château Richeux

Route du Mont-Saint-Michel, 35350 Saint-Méloir-des-Ondes. **Tel: 011 33 2 99 89 64 76.**
Fax: 011 33 2 99 89 88 47. www.maisons-de-bricourt.com info@maisons-de-bricourt.com

An integral part of great French leader Olivier Roellinger's "Maisons de Bricourt," this splendid Belle Epoque manor house offers one of the best views there is of the Mont-Saint-Michel. Thanks to the reflection through bow windows, the bistro, as well as the 10 or so bedrooms, get their colors from the pastel hues of the bay. The mountain rises like a ghost on the horizon, and you get a front-row view from the bed in the "Galanga" room, which is filled with quality Indian furniture.
Blue mosaic and anise for its Art Deco neighbor "Anis Etoilé" ("Starred Anise"), into which light floods through no less than seven windows. And in the dining room, the offerings range from a "Velouté of Velvet Crab" to a serving cart full of grandmother's desserts.

- 11 rooms: $165–$310.
- 2 apartments: $280–$315.
- Breakfast: $17.
- Menus: $25 and $50.
- Open year round.

L'Hôtel Sainte-Marine

Finistère

Mr. Diquélou, 19, rue du Bac. 29120 Sainte-Marine.
Tel: 011 33 2 98 56 34 79. Fax: 011 33 2 98 51 94 09. guy.diquelou@wanadoo.fr

With its terrace overlooking the ocean and its 11 funny little rooms, the Hôtel Sainte-Marine smacks of happiness and vacations in Brittany. The decor is bright and airy: Starfish that make the sandy-colored walls sparkle; furniture picked up from here and there, and painted a glossy, bright color; mosaic and deck floors; bed-covers like weathered sails. Everything here breathes of the sea and bobbing boats. At Sainte-Marine, in this picture-perfect fishing port of slate-roofed white houses, you feel as though you're on an island—but it's the people on the opposite side, in Bénodet, who are the foreigners.

- 11 rooms: $55–$70.
- Breakfast: $10.
- Menus: $20–$50.
- Open year round.

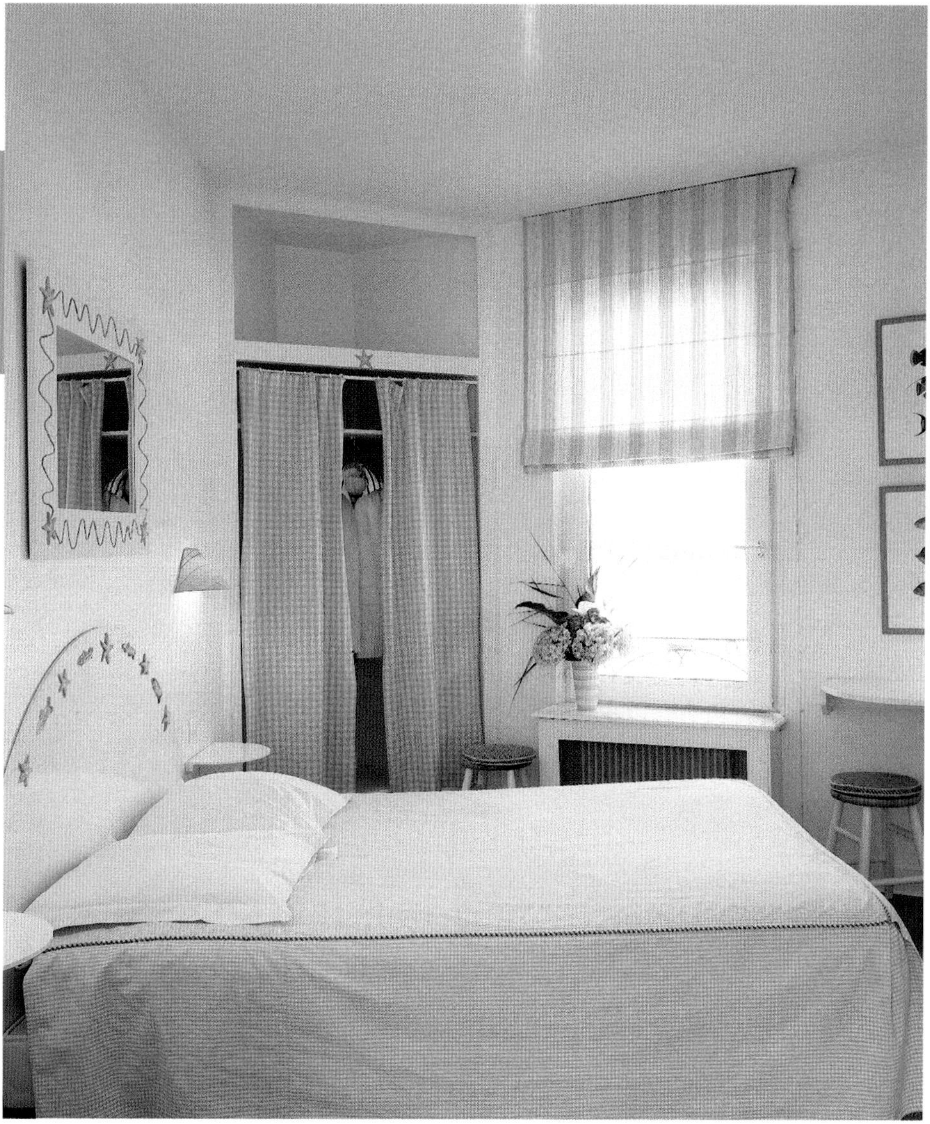

Le Château de Guilguiffin

29710 Landudec. **Tel: 011 33 2 98 91 52 11. Fax: 011 33 2 98 91 52 52.**
www.guilguiffin.com chateau@guilguiffin.com

This old chateau, which owes its reputation to Maximilien Foy, General in Chief of the Napoleonic Artillery, is like something out of a history book: It changed its vocation from one of defense to one of pleasure, influenced by long-distance travelers following the trail of the East India Trading Company years ago. It is via a majestic, granite staircase that you get to the huge bedrooms, revamped and modernized with fabrics created by well-known contemporary designers. The yellow, pink, and blue hues flatter the portraits on the walls, bring out the veins in the marble, and breathe life into the exposed timberwork. A fresco of *Birds of the Marshes* hangs against a background of "crême caramel" paneling. The panes of glass in "La Chapelle" filter the light from the hydrangea-filled garden. Breakfasts, served in front of a gargantuan fireplace in the chateau's kitchen, are a pleasure. And all you have to do is reach for the shelf suspended above the table to grab the homemade jam that goes so well with the Breton cakes.

- 5 rooms: $100–$140.
- 2 suites: $180–$220.
- Breakfast included.
- Closed from November 15 to March 1.

Le Relais du Vieux Port

Finistère

Mr. Quiguiner, 1, quai du Drellac'h, 29217 Le Conquet.
Tel: 011 33 2 98 89 15 91.

A genuine seaside setting for this little hotel, armored in granite and anchored at the port of Conquet, just 330 yards from the take-off point for the islands of Molène and Ouessant. A blue terrace leads you into a traditional crêperie. You can borrow one of their books before going up to one of the seven rooms, with very Atlantic color schemes and shutters that open on to the high seas. Stencils run along the walls, the beds are four-posters and made of wood, and the sheets are crisp white. Whatever the decoration—be it checks, stripes, waves, or seashells—the dominant colors are always the same: blue and white. The whole feeling is invigorating and friendly. And the crêperie on the ground floor can satisfy even the largest of appetites.

- 7 rooms: $40–$60.
- Breakfast: $7.
- Meals: $20.
- Open year round.

La Grange de Coatelan

Mr. and Mrs. de Ternay, 29640 Plougonven.
Tel/fax: 011 33 2 98 72 60 16.

This former grange in Breton country, now a refined, charming inn, is a place where log fires burn year-round in the hearth. Guests gather around candlelit tables laid with blue napkins, while the bar-kitchen conjures Breton specialties and generous mixed salads. There are three guest rooms upstairs. The most original is now where the old pigsty used to be—a box bed is its only rustic feature. A milk cauldron acts as bed canopy, tied with blue-striped drapes. On the floor, cabochon red tiles, Delft-style, lead to the pale wood bathroom where they give way to navy blue earthenware tiles. An old sink and a table made from the stand of a sewing machine lend a retro note, an armchair in wood and steel give a more contemporary feel. On the mezzanine, two children's beds are set beneath a wooden hut and bluish beams.

- 3 rooms: $45–$60.
- Additional bed: $15–$20.
- Breakfast included.
- Meals: $20–$25.
- Closed for Christmas.

Le Château de Lezhildry

Mr. and Mrs. Thomin-O'laughlin, 22220 Plouguiel. **Tel/fax: 011 33 2 96 92 39 37.**
www.au-chateau.com/Lezhildry.htm   Lezhildry.chateau@wanadoo.fr

In this old armory you can still see pieces of ordnance: This noble 14th, 15th, and 16th century residence has not changed much. But its new owners have come to invent a future for it, welcoming guests amid the 21st century comfort of rooms done up in designer fabrics. These re-editions of old fabrics go wonderfully well with the linen sheets, wooden four-poster beds, granite fireplaces, and chestnut ceilings filled with clay and covered with straw and whitewash. They also go well with the hangings, chests, and knickknacks which appear here, there and everywhere—memories of journeys to friendly lands. The place clearly touched the owners with its elegance, so they haven't altered the building's structure. They've even kept the ogive ribs in the kitchen, which you can admire over breakfast. During the summer, though, you'll enjoy breakfast outside under the garden arches.

- 5 rooms: $150–$250.
- Breakfast included.
- Open year round.

Le Char à bancs

Lamour family, Moulin de la Ville Geffroy, 22170 Plélo.
Tel: 011 33 2 96 74 13 63. Fax: 011 33 2 96 74 13 03. charabanc@wanadoo.fr

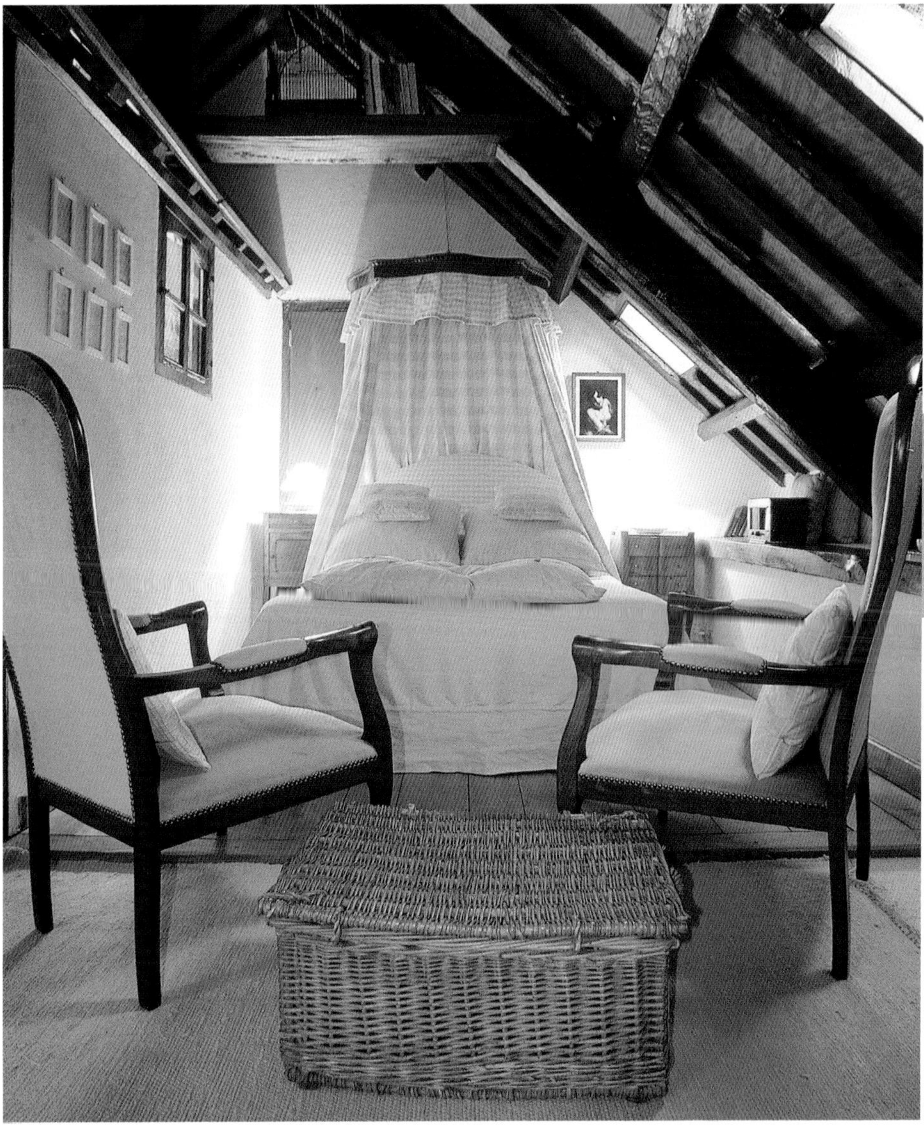

This farmhouse gets its name from the old horse-and-carts that used to take people to Sunday mass. Le Char à bancs has also become synonymous with ecotourism, thanks to a family that has championed the policy for three generations now. This incredibly rustic inn is installed in an old mill down in a tributary of the river Trieux. The guest rooms capture a Breton atmosphere with box beds, old sewing machines, ancestral portraits, heavy lacework, and furniture worthy of any good second-hand store.

- 4 rooms: $65–$85.
- Meals: $15–$30.
- Closed from September 15 to September 30.

Le Domaine de Clairvaux

Calvados

Mr. and Mrs. Crausaz, 14140 Les Moutiers-Hubert.
Tel: 011 33 2 31 32 55 56. Fax: 011 33 2 31 63 68 77. cclairvaux@aol.com

Some years ago, innkeepers Alice and Cyril Crausaz—who is an osteopath for horses—bought this property set in 20 acres of forest. They have turned the former watchman's dwelling into a rural abode. Salmon pink and peacock blue for the curtains, quilted or squared patterns for the bedspreads, these rooms with country furnishings are enhanced by baskets of hydrangeas matching the hues of the bathrooms. The horse rules here, displayed on walls and relaxing as sculptures on pine chests. As a refuge for the weary or a base for hiking, this horseback rider's residence will also appeal to bikers, weekend walkers, and horse-lovers.

- 3 rooms: $55.
- Breakfast included.
- 1 cottage: $600 for a week, breakfast not included.
- Horseback riding.
- Open year round.

Aux Pommiers de Livaye

Mr. and Mrs. Lambert, 14340 Notre-Dame-de-Livaye. **Tel: 011 33 2 31 63 01 28.**
Fax: 011 33 2 31 63 73 63. http://bandb.normandy.free.fr bandb.normandy@free.fr

Behind the woodland and climbing roses, at the end of a carriage drive, you'll find this country inn. Inside, watercolors remind us that Impressionism was born around the corner. Opening the linen curtains, you'll glimpse cows grazing beneath apple trees—a picture-postcard Normandy that recurs in the romantic decor of the bedrooms, where roses and wisteria cling to the timberwork. Bunches of hydrangeas on chests-of-drawers and books on bedside tables greet guests of "Famille Tendresse," a room done in fuchsia. "Reine des champs" is decorated in soft green, while "Haut des Pommiers" filled with flowers, is just off the spiral staircase. And, in the dining room, the Lamberts serve up a menu of local fare.

- 6 rooms: $70–$140.
- Breakfast included.
- Meals: starting at $25.
- Closed from December 1 to March 1

La Réserve

Eure

Didier and Marie-Lorraine Brunet, 27620 Giverny.
Tel/fax: 011 33 2 32 21 99 09. www.giverny.org/hotels/brunet ml1reserve@aol.com

Innkeeper Didier Brunet designed it; his wife Marie-Lorraine decorated it. The main building conjures Monet's house, which is located nearby. Behind its saffron-yellow façade surmounted by russet tiles from Burgundy, a series of lounges and dining rooms lets light filter in through the inn's tall windows. With all its influences and recycled materials, you'd imagine the house, built just a few years ago, would be somewhat soulless and homogeneous. The very opposite is true: It has a strong personality, and is unforgettable with its pale woodwork, hunting trophies used as coat racks, orchard aromas, and bold colors in blue, slate-gray, dark red, peony, cream, and indigo. The most amazing of the rooms is done in sepia. In the bathrooms, you'll find monogrammed towels and oat-scented soap.

- 5 rooms: $85–$145.
- Breakfast included.
- Open year round.

Eure

Les Saisons

27400 Vironvay.
Tel: 011 33 2 32 40 02 56. Fax: 011 33 2 32 25 05 26.

Just a stone's throw from the Val de Seine, this estate was actually a stud farm in the early 20th century. Today, the façades of the small pink brick houses, crisscrossed with blue timberwork, hide 10 comfy rooms with a mix of flowers, tiles, carefully selected madras cottons, and English furniture. The hues of pink, bright anise-green, and buttercup enhance the quilted fabrics and the mats of woolly coir. A farmyard supplies the table with fresh eggs, a vegetable garden with early produce, an orchard with fruit, and a garden with herbs. It's no surprise that chef Henry-Louis Portier is well-known in Normandy's gastronomic circles.
In summer evenings, dinner is served by candlelight under the weeping willow in the yard.

- 6 rooms: $73–$140.
- 4 suites: $145–$235.
- Breakfast: $15.
- Menus: starting at $35.
- Pool, tennis.
- Closed for Christmas and in February.

La Gribane

Michèle and Jean-Pierre Douchet, 297, quai Jeanne d'Arc, 80230 Saint-Valéry-sur-Somme. **Tel: 011 33 3 22 60 97 55.**

This is a beautiful villa set on an embankment at the mouth of the River Somme, a building where servants were housed in the 1930s. Owners Michèle and Jean-Pierre Douchet have transformed it into a 21st century vacation spot set in a huge garden overflowing with perennials. The inn houses a suite done in all pastels. Small hurricane lamps in zinc and wood, carpets with sailing-ship hues—the decor is in harmony with what you see out the inn's windows. A beautiful sisal carpet and a collection of gulls on the pretty chest-of-drawers in the second suite take on the same soft, azure and slate-blue hues.

- 2 rooms: $65.
- 2 suites: $75.
- Breakfast included.
- Open year round.

L'Auberge de la Grenouillère

La Madelaine-sous-Montreuil, 62170 Montreuil-sur-Mer. **Tel: 011 33 3 21 06 07 22.**
Fax: 011 33 3 21 86 36 36. www.lagrenouillere.fr auberge.de.la grenouillere@wanadoo.fr

The banks of the Canche and the Course are lined with small white houses that resemble Irish cottages. The Auberge de la Grenouillère is one of them, with its little courtyard tables set with flowers.

La Grenouillère's decor can be called amphibious: Frogs have taken over, from the floor tiles to the wallpaper. Chef Roland Gauthier swears that they're gifts from former guests. The centerpiece of the collection are the dining room frescoes, which English humorist Frank Reynolds put there in 1925. They tell the tale of a flirtatious frog and a self-satisfied toad. And the bedrooms? They're very spring-like, with floral fabrics, marsh-green hues, and lacework, all underpinned by airy watercolors and strangely appropriate plant illustrations.

■ 4 rooms: $75–$95.
■ Breakfast: $10.
■ Meals: $30–$65.
■ Closed in January.

Station Bac Saint-Maur

77, rue de la Gare, 62840 Sailly-sur-la-Lys. **Tel: 011 33 3 21 02 68 20.**
Fax: 011 33 3 21 02 74 37. perso.wanadoo.fr/station-bac-saint-maur/ chefdegare@wanadoo.fr

This is a unique place: An enthusiastic young couple decided to renovate an old PLM railcar—Paris-Lyons-Marseilles—and turn an abandoned railway station into a Flemish inn. To do so, they revamped the decor of the car with sycamore wood inlaid with mother-of-pearl and mahogany marquetry, repaired the small bedside reading lamps, and repolished the beveled mirrors of the basin units. Two showers and lavatories in the corridor serve the six cabins. Motionless travelers on this unusual journey back through time are awakened by the light that filters through sliding curtains every morning. And if you feel like dining in the restaurant car, you'll be served by the station-master, in full uniform.

- 6 cabins, each for 2 people: $40–$65.
- Breakfast: $7.
- Menus: $10–$25.
- Closed from November 1 to March 31.

LENS
DOUAI
VALENCIENNES
ARRAS
CAMBRAI
AVESNES-SUR-HELPE
0
50
100 km
PERONNE
SAINT-QUENTIN
CHARLEVILLE-MEZIERES
VERVINS
MONTDIDIER
SEDAN
PICARDIE
LAON
RETHEL
CLERMONT
Oise
VOUZIERS
Meuse
THIONVILLE
COMPIEGNE
SOISSONS
Saint-Thierry
BOULAY-MOSELLE
BRIEY
La Ferté-Milon
REIMS
SAINTE-MENEHOULD
FORBACH
SENLIS
VERDUN
METZ
SARREGUEMINES
CHATEAU-THIERRY
Marne
EPERNAY
Moselle
WISSEMBOURG
CHALONS-EN-CHAMPAGNE
MEAUX
Etoges
LORRAINE
CHATEAU-SALINS
HAGUENAU
VITRY-LE-FRANÇOIS
SAVERNE
COMMERCY
NANCY
SARREBOURG
ILE-DE-FRANCE
BAR-LE-DUC
STRASBOURG
TOUL
LUNEVILLE
MOLSHEIM
PROVINS
SAINT-DIZIER
Seine
Aube
MELUN
ALSACE
NOGENT-SUR-SEINE
FONTAINEBLEAU
CHAMPAGNE-ARDENNE
Meurthe
SAINT-DIE
SELESTAT
NEUFCHATEAU
Les Rouges-Eaux
TROYES
RIBEAUVILLE
Rhin
SENS
EPINAL
Bulgneville
Gérardmer
BAR-SUR-AUBE
CHAUMONT
COLMAR
Ventron
Eguisheim
GUEBWILLER
MONTARGIS
THANN
LANGRES
MULHOUSE
AUXERRE
LURE
BELFORT
VESOUL
ALTKIRCH
MONTBARD
Saône
FRANCHE-COMTE
MONTBELIARD
AVALLON
CLAMECY
Yonne
COSNE-SUR-LOIRE
DIJON
BESANÇON
BOURGOGNE
Doubs
La Longeville
BOURGES
CHATEAU-CHINON
DOLE
AUTUN
BEAUNE
Montbenoît
NEVERS
PONTARLIER
CHALON-SUR-SAONE
SAINT-AMAND-MONTROND
LONS-LE-SAUNIER
Ain
MOULINS
LOUHANS
Lac Léman
CHAROLLES
SAINT-CLAUDE
GEX
Rhône
Saône
THONON-LES-BAINS
MONTLUÇON
MACON
Allier

East

Le Château d'Etoges
51270 Etoges.

Le Clos du Mont d'Hor
51220 Saint-Thierry.

L'Hôtel Racine
02460 La Ferté-Milon.

L'Hostellerie du Château
68420 Eguisheim.

Le Chalet de l'Epinette
88400 Gérardmer.

Les Bas-Rupts
88400 Gérardmer.

Le Grand Hôtel
88400 Gérardmer.

La Cholotte
88600 Les Rouges-Eaux.

Les Buttes
88310 Ventron.

Maison d'Hôtes de Bulgneville
88140 Bulgneville.

Chez les Colin
25650 Montbenoît.

Le Crêt l'Agneau
25650 La Longeville.

Le Château d'Etoges

4, rue Richebourg, 51270 Etoges. **Tel: 011 33 3 26 59 30 08. Fax: 011 33 3 26 59 35 57.**
www.etoges.com etoges@wanadoo.fr

With its large plump towers set in a moat, this stout old castle has something comforting about it. It was used as a staging post for France's kings and was even linked to Napoleon before falling into neglect. Nowadays it offers visitors comfort and elegance along with its medieval history in rooms and suites located just off a stone staircase. There's something to suit all tastes here, from the prestigious Empire room to the former maid's bedrooms with their bull's-eye windows; from rustic rooms where butterflies play into the decor to romantic rooms where you sleep beneath muslin-shrouded canopies. Then there are colonial rooms and country rooms clad in toile de Jouy and decorated with stencils. Add in the ducks bobbing on the moat, a barge which acts as a gondola, and the vineyards visible from the rooftop, and this is a castle setting not soon forgotten.

- 10 rooms: $90–$230.
- Breakfast: $15.
- Menus: $30–$60.
- Closed a few weeks in January and February.

Le Clos du Mont d'Hor

Marne

Nicolas and Antoine Lemaire, 8, rue du Mont d'Hor, 51220 Saint-Thierry.
Tel: 011 33 3 26 03 12 42. Fax: 011 33 3 26 03 02 80. montdhor@ebc.net

The young owners of this farming estate were intent on shattering its traditional image. And they've succeeded: Six guest rooms have been installed in old sheep-folds, partitioned behind a poppy-red wall. The first room uses a piece of a ship as a headboard. The second, "Coloniale," is draped beneath a mosquito net and surrounded by Indonesian furniture. In the bathroom, an orange tub with lion's feet presents the Baroque ambience of "A Thousand and One Nights" with a bed set beneath a moiré-patterned polonaise. Its bathroom has a New York-loft feel, with white imitation brickwork everywhere. The last room offers a Zen-like atmosphere, truly Japanese in style. And all the rooms look out over the vineyards of Champagne.

- 5 suites and 1 room with facilities for the disabled: $80.
- Additional bed: $17.
- Breakfast: $8.
- Open year round.

Aisne

L'Hôtel Racine

Liliane Waterlot, place du Port-au-blé, 02460 La Ferté-Milon. **Tel: 011 33 3 23 96 72 02.**
Fax: 011 33 3 23 96 72 37. iap@club-internet.fr

This is a dwelling of writers— where Racine's grandmother lived, where La Fontaine was married in 1647, and where current owner Liliane Waterlot decided to set up a painting school run by artists and Fine Arts teachers.
From the start, the loft was turned into a studio, and the hotel has bustled beneath it. In a Baroque atmosphere, the living room is adorned with abstract and figurative canvases and tawny leather sofas.
Eight comfortable bedrooms, reached by way of a 16th century staircase, welcome travelers and amateur artists alike.
At breakfast, the straw-and tea-rose-colored dining room is an island of light. The cobbled courtyard, opening onto a garden by the canal banks, invites visitors to take a walk.

- 8 rooms: $50–$60.
- Breakfast: $8.
- Open year round.

L'Hostellerie du Château

2, place du château Saint-Léon IX, 68420 Eguisheim. **Tel: 011 33 3 89 23 72 00.**
Fax: 011 33 3 89 41 63 93. www.hostellerieduchateau.com info@hostellerieduchateau.com

This small hotel opens its green shutters onto one of the prettiest squares in this wine country. Above the reception desk, three zinc clocks tell you the time in the world's largest metropolises. A spirit of open-mindedness comes through in the decor: canvases signed by contemporary artists and a large wooden statue in the shape of a goddess, which was carved with a chainsaw. In the rooms, headboards are made of varnished chipboard, and the cupboard doors and parts of the walls are made of recycled wood. The furniture is reduced to raw materials: the bedside lamps are in rusted metal, and the trilogy of colors are kept to almond green, ultramarine, and pumpkin-orange. In summer, breakfast is served beneath parasols in the shadow of an old, imposing castle.

- 11 rooms: $65–$120.
- Breakfast: $10.
- Closed from January 1 to February 15.

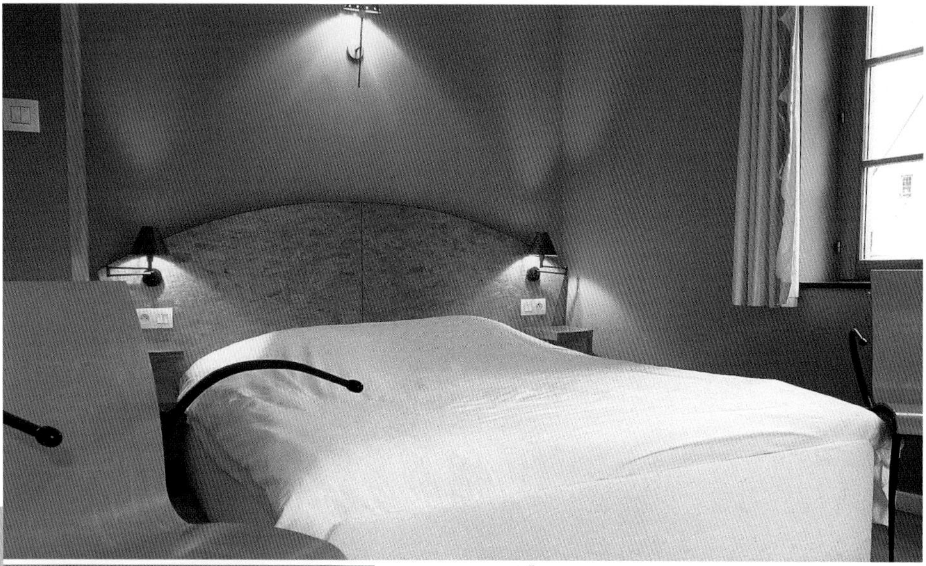

Le Chalet de l'Epinette

Gisèle and Claudine Poirot-Scherrer, 70, chemin de la Trinité, 88400 Gérardmer.
Tel/fax: 011 33 3 29 63 40 06. epinette@libertysurf.fr

This is a large, orange wooden chalet on a hill in the town of Gérardmer. Through its windows, the view takes in peaks covered in large firs. You'll be welcomed by innkeeper Claudine Poirot-Scherrer and her daughter Gisèle, as well as by the sweet and spicy aromas wafting from the kitchen. An array of some 50 jars of homemade jam, many in exotic flavors, won't disappoint. But tear yourself from the table to see the rooms: Rustic and romantic, their sunny decor is helped along by bunches of forget-me-nots and rooms filled with light.

- Rooms: $53–$59.
- Breakfast included.
- Meals: $20.
- Sauna.
- Accessible to the disabled.
- Closed from November 18 to December 6.

Les Bas-Rupts

Mr. and Mrs. Philippe, 181, route de la Bresse, 88400 Gérardmer. **Tel: 011 33 3 29 63 09 25.**
Fax: 011 33 3 29 63 00 40. www.bas-rupts.com bas-rupts@wanadoo.fr

You'll experience true tranquility in this "house of silence," situated on a mountainside at the gateway to Gérardmer. Old wooden sleds nailed to the walls of this chalet help set the tone. Blonde wood, doors painted in the Eastern style, thistles carved in friezes, fabrics with mixed flowers and checks in brick-red and saffron tones, golden-yellow walls, and currant-red carpets all play a part in completing this comfy, cozy atmosphere. Les Bas-Rupts is also known for its gourmet food: The buffet breakfast offered in the dining room, with its large windows and lovely views, is a treat.

- 24 rooms and suites: \$110–\$215.
- Half-board: \$125–\$185.
- Breakfast: \$15.
- Meals: \$40–\$80.
- Pool.
- Tennis.
- Open year round.

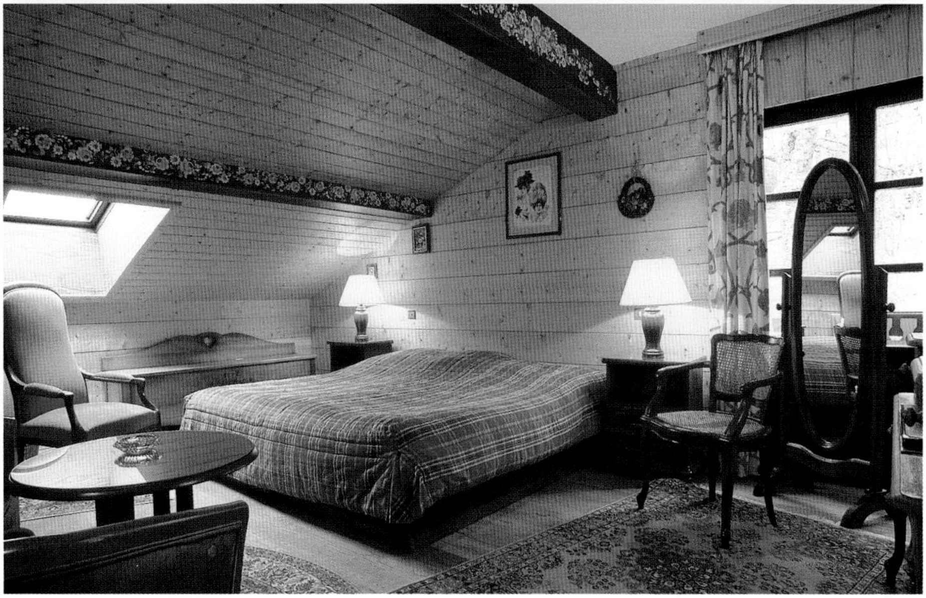

Le Grand Hôtel

Place du Tilleul, B.P. 12, 88401 Gérardmer. **Tel: 011 33 3 29 63 06 31.**
Fax: 011 33 3 29 63 46 81. www.grandhotel-gerardmer.com gerardmer-grandhotel@wanadoo.fr

This place has seen two centuries of history pass by. First there was the rich Alsatian who founded it in 1870. It was turned into a hospital during one war and then saw troops head to battle in World War II. In 1966, a businessman bought it and made it the showroom for his textiles company. Today it's in the hands of Claude Rémy and his wife, who've transformed it into a hotel which has managed to evolve with the times. The rooms, clad in golden yellow, pale green, raspberry, and brick-red, are accompanied by bathrooms, with the most striking caramel marbling.

- 68 rooms: $70–$105.
- 4 suites: $140.
- Breakfast included.
- Menus: starting at $25.
- Half-board: starting at $70.
- Pool.
- Open year round.

La Cholotte

Marie-Geneviève Cholé, 88600 Les Rouges-Eaux.
Tel: 011 33 3 29 50 56 93. Fax: 011 33 3 29 50 24 12.

Combining catering, the hotel trade, gardening, culture, and life in the middle of the forest was Marie-Geneviève Cholé's dream. She has a certain flair for drama, such as scattering flower petals all over the tables, and creating new, innovative dishes for an autumn menu, such as mushrooms with pumpkin. Her specialty is a whole ham cooked in meadow hay. You'll try the year's new wine as an *apéritif*, accompanied by a basket of walnuts. The rooms are all mixed metaphors: A dash of the 18th century here, a tad classical there, and then romantic with green ginghams and a frieze of pink ribbons in one of the bedrooms. Yet in another room with creamy ivory-colored planks on the floor and white furniture, the spirit is unabashedly "trendy."

- 5 rooms: $73.
- Breakfast: $10.
- Closed from November 15 to January 31.

Les Buttes

Thibaut Leduc, 88310 Ventron.
Tel: 011 33 3 29 24 18 09. Fax: 011 33 3 29 24 21 96. www.frerejo.com

This out-of-the-ordinary hotel, renovated head to toe in 2000, is in the mountains of the Vosges range, a stone's throw from the hermitage of Brother Joseph. A family of hoteliers took over the site from him, then proceeded to contribute 11 children to the French skiing team from the 1940s to the 1960s! Thibaut Leduc, who bought the hotel a few years ago, has endowed it with a homey comfort. The new rooms are wrapped in warm autumn hues. Saffron tablecloths with cranberry designs appear in the pale yellow dining room. It's also worth noting that in winter, the ski trails at this family resort—where children are more than welcome—come right down to the doors of the hotel.

- 27 rooms: $75–$170.
- Meals: $25.
- Pool, sauna, Jacuzzi.
- Closed from November 15 to December 15.

Maison d'Hôtes de Bulgnéville

Vosges

Mr. Benoit Breton, 74, rue des Recollets, 88140 Bulgnéville.
Tel/fax: 011 33 3 29 09 21 72. Benoit.Breton@wanadoo.fr

Near Vittel, this beautiful family home with green shutters is surrounded by pink hydrangeas. Restored by a pair of antiques dealers, this hotel's furniture is sure to impress: A small Louis XVI chair with stencil-painted fabric for a room covered in white, ivory, and cream hues against an almond-green carpet; a Napoleon III settee for another room, with its soft pearl and lilac hues; and chandeliers hanging above a round table of gray-veined marble for a third, further complemented by sunny tones. A bathroom with blue *azulejos* tiles and white and caramel marble for a fourth bedroom, done in azure and sunflower. And the breakfast room may beckon you to bargain hunt, as everything in it is for sale.

- 4 rooms: $70–$85.
- Breakfast included.
- Closed for Christmas.

Doubs

Chez les Colin

Hauterive, La Fresse, 25650 Montbenoît.
Tel/fax: 011 33 3 81 46 51 63.

This old custom's house is situated on one of the folds of the Jura mountains, where the innkeepers, a former businessman and a nurse, make their own jams with melon, fresh mint, pears, and walnuts. The refined rooms are decorated in the gentle, pale yellow harmony of Franche-Comté furniture, which goes well with all the old knick knacks: a water pitcher, an old-fashioned vase, lace curtains, and bird screens. The same comfy atmosphere reigns in the lounge, where mountainous views are enjoyed. Overnight guests share showers and toilets, but there are sinks in every room. In winter, cross-country ski trails are right outside. In the summer, easels are set up in nearby meadows for watercolor courses.

- 6 rooms.
- Full-board: $500 for a week.
- Cross-country ski equipment included.
- Summer: $450 for a week.
- Closed in May, June, October, and November.

Le Crêt l'Agneau

Les Auberges, 25650 La Longeville. **Tel: 011 33 3 81 38 12 51.**
Fax: 011 33 3 81 38 16 58. www.lecret-lagneau.com contact@lecret-lagneau.com

Don't be surprised if you cross paths with a couple of roe deer, or hares, or even stray foxes on a cross-country ski jaunt through Jura country. Then, after a morning spent on the move, you'll stop for a picnic: Mont-d'Or cheese washed down with Jura wine and potatoes cooked in embers. All you have to do is cut a few branches and light the fire. And in the evening, after some more cross-country skiing, the gourmet cuisine will replenish you. Le Crêt l'Agneau is a 17th century Franche-Comté farm, with its cedar fireplace typical of the region and seven guest rooms, each with its own bathroom. Hikers and skiers are welcomed to overnight in a setting of sleigh beds covered with fat eiderdowns. The charm of this house is in the simple things: the aroma of grilled bread wafting from the oven, and an amazing range of homemade jams.

- 7 rooms: $60–$65.
- Cross-country package, 6 days with full board: $500–$600, equipment included.
- Open year round.

Index by "départements"

Aisne (02)
L'Hôtel Racine, La Ferté-Milon, **p. 144**

Allier (03)
Le Manoir de La Mothe, Vicq, **p. 104**

Alpes-de-Haute-Provence (04)
Le Vivier, Enchastrayes, **p. 34**

Alpes-Maritimes (06)
Le Mas Samarcande, Golfe-Juan-Vallauris, **p. 10**
Le Bosquet, Antibes-Juan-les-Pins, **p. 11**
La Roseraie, Vence, **p. 12**
La Villa Estelle, Haut-de-Cagnes, **p. 13**

Ardèche (07)
La Santoline, Beaulieu, **p. 32**
Le Couradou, Labastide-de-Virac, **p. 33**

Aude (11)
Le Grand Guilhem, Cascastel, **p. 46**
Le Domaine du Haut-Gléon, Durban, **p. 47**
La Mignoterie, Fajac-en-Val, **p. 48**

Aveyron (12)
La Méjanassère, Entraygues, **p. 49**
La Ferme de Moulhac, Laguiole, **p. 50**
L'Hôtel du Vieux Pont, Belcastel, **p. 51**
La Musardière, Millau, **p. 52**

Bouches-du-Rhône (13)
Le Jardin d'Émile, Cassis, **p. 17**
Le Mas dou Pastre, Eygalières, **p. 18**
Aux Deux Sœurs, Saint-Étienne-du-Grès, **p. 19**
Le Calendal, Arles, **p. 20**
La Maison d'Hôtes, Tarascon, **p. 21**
Le Mas des Arnajons, Le Puy-Sainte-Réparade, **p. 22**
La Haute Terre, Saint-Antonin-sur-Bayon, **p. 23**

Calvados (14)
Le Domaine de Clairvaux, Les Moutiers-Hubert, **p. 133**
Aux Pommiers de Livaye, Notre-Dame-de-Livaye, **p. 134**

Charente (16)
Le Château de Maumont, Magnac-sur-Touvre, **p. 90**
Le Logis du Portal, Vars, **p. 91**

Charente-Maritime (17)
L'Hôtel de l'Océan, Le Bois-Plage-en-Ré, **p. 87**
Le Chat Botté, Saint-Clément-des-Baleines, **p. 88**
La Maison Douce, Saint-Martin-de-Ré, **p. 89**

Cher (18)
La Reculée en Berry, Montigny, **p. 105**
Le Domaine de la Trolière, Orval, **p. 106**
Les Bonnets Rouges, Bourges, **p. 107**

Corrèze (19)
La Maison, Beaulieu-sur-Dordogne, **p. 94**

Haute-Corse (20)
La Villa Calvi, Calvi, **p. 53**
La Signoria, Calvi, **p. 54**
La Casa Musicale, Pigna, **p. 55**
La Casa Corsa, Cervione, **p. 56**
Castel Brando, Erbalunga, **p. 57**

Côte-d'Or (21)
La Villa Louise, Aloxe-Corton, **p. 103**

Côtes-d'Armor (22)
Le Château de Lezhildry, Plouguiel, **p. 131**
Le Char à bancs, Plélo, **p. 132**

Creuse (23)
Les Vergnes, Saint-Pardoux-le-Neuf, **p. 95**
Château de la Chassagne, Saint-Hilaire-le-Château, **p. 96**

Dordogne (24)
Le Chaufourg, Sourzac, **p. 64**

Doubs (25)
Chez les Colin, Montbenoit, **p. 152**
Le Crêt l'Agneau, La Longeville, **p. 153**

Drôme (26)
La Treille Muscate, Cliousclat, **p. 27**
Une Autre Maison, Nyons, **p. 28**
La Maison Forte de Clérivaux, Châtillon-Saint-Jean, **p. 29**
La Maison de Soize, Colonzelle, **p. 30**
Le Clair de Plume, Grignan, **p. 31**

Eure (27)
La Réserve, Giverny, **p. 135**
Les Saisons, Vironvay, **p. 136**

Finistère (29)
L'Hôtel Sainte-Marine, Sainte-Marine, **p. 127**
Le Château de Guilguiffin, Landudec, **p. 128**
Le Relais du Vieux Port, Le Conquet, **p. 129**
La Grange de Coatelan, Plougonven, **p. 130**

Gard (30)
Le Château de Saint-Maximin, Saint-Maximin, **p. 40**
Le Mas de l'Amandier, Ribaute-les-Tavernes, **p. 41**

Gers (32)
La Lumiane, Saint-Puy, **p. 66**
Le Moulin de Régis, Mirande, **p. 67**

Gironde (33)
La Maison du Bassin, Lège-Cap-Ferret, **p. 86**

Ille-et-Vilaine (35)
La Filanderie, Bécherel, **p. 123**
Lecoq-Gadby, Rennes, **p. 124**
Le Château de la Ballue, Bazouges-la-Pérouse, **p. 125**
Le Château Richeux, Saint-Méloir-des-Ondes, **p. 126**

Indre-et-Loire (37)
Le Château des Réaux, Chouzé-sur-Loire, **p. 108**
Le Domaine des Bidaudières, Vouvray, **p. 109**
Le Château de Montgouverne, Rochecorbon, **p. 110**

Landes (40)

Pain, Adour et Fantaisie, Grenade-sur-l'Adour, **p. 82**
Capcazal de Pachiou, Mimbaste, **p. 83**
Ty Gias, Seignosse, **p. 84**
Les Hortensias du Lac, Hossegor, **p. 85**

Loir-et-Cher (41)

Le Manoir de Clénord, Mont-près-Chambord, **p. 111**

Loire (42)

L'Echauguette, Saint-Jean-Saint-Maurice-sur-Loire, **p. 101**

Haute-Loire (43)

Les Deux Abbesses, Saint-Arcons-d'Allier, **p. 100**

Loiret (45)

Les Courtils, Chécy, **p. 112**
La Ferme des Foucault, Ménestreau-en-Villette, **p. 113**

Lot (46)

Le Château de la Treyne, Lacave, **p. 60**
La Pelissaria, Saint-Cirq-Lapopie, **p. 61**
Le Mas Azémar, Mercuès, **p. 62**

Lot-et-Garonne (47)

Le Moulin de Labique, Villeréal, **p. 65**

Maine-et-Loire (49)

Le Château de Noirieux, Briollay, **p. 118**
Le Domaine de Mestre, Fontevraud-l'Abbaye, **p. 119**

Marne (51)

Le Château d'Etoges, Étoges, **p. 142**
Le Clos du Mont d'Hor, Saint-Thierry, **p. 143**

Nord-Pas-de-Calais (62)

L'Auberge de la Grenouillère, Montreuil-sur-Mer, **p. 138**
Station Bac Saint-Maur, Sailly-sur-la-Lys, **p. 139**

Puy-de-Dôme (63)

Le Chastel Montaigu, Montaigut-le-Blanc, **p 97**
La Vigie, Chadeleuf, **p. 98**
Le Moulin de Vernières, Aubusson-d'Auvergne, **p. 99**

Pyrénées-Atlantiques (64)

La Ferme Dagué, Lasseube, **p. 70**
Le Domaine de Pédelaborde, Poey-d'Oloron, **p. 71**
L'Oustalet, Accous, **p. 72**
Le Relais Linague, Urcuit, **p. 73**
La Maison Sainbois, La Bastide-Clairence, **p. 74**
La Croisade, La Bastide-Clairence, **p. 75**
Olhabidea, Sare, **p. 76**
La Maison Irigoïan, Bidart, **p. 77**
Aretxola, Sare, **p. 78**
Irazabala, Espelette, **p. 79**
La Devinière, Saint-Jean-de-Luz, **p. 80**
Maison Cap Blanc, Monségur, **p. 81**

Hautes-Pyrénées (65)

Les Musardises, Fontrailles, **p. 68**
Eth Beyre Petit, Beaucens, **p. 69**

Pyrénées-Orientales (66)

Le Mas Bazan, Alénya, **p. 42**
Laurence Jonquères d'Oriola, Corneilla-del-Vercol, **p. 43**
La Vieille Demeure, Torreilles, **p. 44**
La Villa Duflot, Perpignan, **p. 45**

Haut-Rhin (68)

L'Hostellerie du Château, Eguisheim, **p. 145**

Saône-et-Loire (71)

La Chaumière, Baudrières, **p. 102**

Sarthe (72)

L'Abbaye de Champagne, Rouez-en-Champagne, **p. 120**
Le Château de Saint-Paterne, Saint-Paterne, **p. 121**
La Seigneurie des Claies, Asnières-sur-Vègre, **p. 122**

Savoie (73)

Hôtel Saint-Martin, Saint-Martin-de-Belleville, **p. 39**

Haute-Savoie (74)

La Crémerie du Glacier, Chamonix, **p. 35**
Les Servages, Les Carroz d'Arâches, **p. 36**
L'Hôtel des Cîmes, Le Grand-Bornand, **p. 37**
Le Chalet-hôtel de la Croix-Fry, Manigod, **p. 38**

Somme (80)

La Gribane, Saint-Valéry-sur-Somme, **p. 137**

Tarn (81)

Les Vents Bleus, Donnazac, **p. 63**

Var (83)

La Bastide rose, Bormes-les-Mimosas, **p. 14**
La Grande Maison, Bormes-les-Mimosas, **p. 15**
L'Hostellerie de l'Abbaye de La Celle, La Celle, **p. 16**

Vaucluse (84)

La Maison, Beaumont du-Ventoux, **p. 24**
La Grange de Jusalem, Mazan, **p. 25**
La Bastide de Marie, Ménerbes, **p. 26**

Vendée (85)

Le Logis de la Cornelière, Mervent, **p. 117**

Vienne (86)

Le Lyon d'Or, Angles-sur-l'Anglin, **p. 116**

Vosges (88)

Le Chalet de l'Epinette, Gérardmer, **p. 146**
Les Bas-Rupts, Gérardmer, **p. 147**
Le Grand Hôtel, Gérardmer, **p. 148**
La Cholotte, Les Rouges-Eaux, **p. 149**
Les Buttes, Ventron, **p. 150**
La Maison d'Hôtes de Bulgnéville, Bulgnéville, **p. 151**

Index by price range

$40–$65

Southeast

Le Calendal,
13200 Arles, **p. 20**
La Maison,
84340 Beaumont-du-Ventoux, **p. 24**
La Treille Muscate,
26270 Cliousclat, **p. 27**
La Maison Forte de Clérivaux,
26750 Châtillon-Saint-Jean, **p. 29**
La Santoline,
07460 Beaulieu, **p. 32**
Le Vivier,
04400 Enchastrayes, **p. 34**
La Crémerie du Glacier,
74400 Chamonix, **p. 35**
Le Mas de l'Amandier,
30720 Ribaute-les-Tavernes, **p. 41**
Le Mas Bazan,
66200 Alénya, **p. 42**
Laurence Jonquères d'Oriola,
66200 Corneilla-del-Vercol, **p. 43**
Le Grand Guilhem,
11360 Cascastel, **p. 46**
La Mignoterie,
11220 Fajac-en-Val, **p. 48**
La Méjanassère,
12140 Entraygues, **p. 49**
La Ferme de Moulhac,
12210 Laguiole, **p. 50**
La Casa Musicale,
20220 Pigna, **p. 55**
La Casa Corsa,
20221 Cervione, **p. 56**

Southwest

Eth Beyre Petit,
65400 Beaucens, **p. 69**
La Ferme Dagué,
64290 Lasseube, **p. 70**
Le Domaine de Pédelaborde,
64400 Poey-d'Oloron, **p. 71**
L'Oustalet,
64490 Accous, **p. 72**
Le Relais Linague,
64990 Urcuit, **p. 73**
La Maison Sainbois,
64240 La Bastide-Clairence, **p. 74**
La Croisade,
64240 La Bastide-Clairence, **p. 75**
Olhabidea,
64310 Sare, **p. 76**
Aretxola,
64130 Sare, **p. 78**
Irazabala,
64250 Espelette, **p. 79**
Maison Cap Blanc,
64460 Monségur, **p. 81**
Capcazal de Pachiou,
40350 Mimbaste, **p. 83**
Ty Gias,
40510 Seignosse, **p. 84**
L'Hôtel de l'Océan,
17580 Le Bois-Plage-en-Ré, **p. 87**
Le Chat Botté,
17590 Saint-Clément-des-Baleines, **p. 88**

Centre-Auvergne

La Maison,
19120 Beaulieu-sur-Dordogne, **p. 94**
Les Vergnes,
23200 Saint-Pardoux-le-Neuf, **p. 95**
La Vigie,
63320 Chadeleuf, **p. 98**
Le Moulin de Vernières,
63120 Aubusson-d'Auvergne, **p. 99**
L'Echauguette,
42155 Saint-Jean-Saint-Maurice-sur-Loire, **p. 101**
La Chaumière,
71370 Baudrières, **p. 102**
La Reculée en Berry,
18250 Montigny, **p. 105**
Le Domaine de la Trolière,
18200 Orval, **p. 106**
Les Bonnets Rouges,
18000 Bourges, **p. 107**
Les Courtils,
45430 Chécy, **p. 112**

West and North

Le Lyon d'Or,
86260 Angles-sur-l'Anglin, **p. 116**
Le Domaine de Mestre,
49590 Fontevraud-l'Abbaye, **p. 119**
L'Abbaye de Champagne,
72140 Rouez-en-Champagne, **p. 120**
La Filanderie,
35190 Bécherel, **p. 123**
L'Hôtel Sainte-Marine,
29120 Sainte-Marine, **p. 127**
Le Relais du Vieux Port,
29217 Le Conquet, **p. 129**
La Grange de Coatelan,
29640 Plougonven, **p. 130**
Le Domaine de Clairvaux,
14140 Les Moutiers-Hubert, **p. 133**
Station Bac Saint-Maur,
62840 Sailly-sur-la-Lys, **p. 139**

East

L'Hôtel Racine,
02460 La Ferté-Milon, **p. 144**
Le Chalet de l'Epinette,
88400 Gérardmer, **p. 146**

$65–$100

Southeast

Le Bosquet,
06160 Antibes-Juan-les-Pins, **p. 11**
La Roseraie,
06140 Vence, **p. 12**
La Bastide rose,
83230 Bormes-les-Mimosas, **p. 14**
La Grande Maison,
83230 Bormes-les-Mimosas, **p. 15**
Le Jardin d'Emile,
13260 Cassis, **p. 17**
Le Mas dou Pastre,
13810 Eygalières, **p. 18**
La Maison d'Hôtes,
13150 Tarascon, **p. 21**
Le Mas des Arnajons,
13610 Le Puy-Sainte-Réparade, **p. 22**
La Grange de Jusalem,
84380 Mazan, **p. 25**
La Maison de Soize,
26230 Colonzelle, **p. 30**
Le Clair de Plumo,
26230 Grignan, **p. 31**
Le Couradou,
07150 Labastide-de-Virac, **p. 33**
L'Hôtel des Cîmes,
74450 Le Grand-Bornand, **p. 37**
Hôtel Saint-Martin,
73440 Saint-Martin-de-Belleville, **p. 39**
La Vieille Demeure,
66440 Torreilles, **p. 44**
Le Domaine du Haut-Gléon,
11360 Durban, **p. 47**
L'Hôtel du Vieux-Pont,
12390 Belcastel, **p. 51**
La Musardière,
12100 Millau, **p. 52**
Castel Brando,
20222 Erbalunga, **p. 57**

Southwest

La Pelissaria,
46330 Saint-Cirq-Lapopie, **p. 61**
Le Mas Azémar,
46090 Mercuès, **p. 62**
Les Vents Bleus,
81170 Donnazac, **p. 63**
Le Moulin de Labique,
47210 Villeréal, **p. 65**
La Lumiane,
32310 Saint-Puy, **p. 66**
Le Moulin de Régis,
32300 Mirande, **p. 67**
Les Musardises,
65220 Fontrailles, **p. 68**
La Maison Irigoïan,
64210 Bidart, **p. 77**
Pain, Adour et Fantaisie,
40270 Grenade-sur-l'Adour, **p. 82**
Les Hortensias du Lac,
40150 Hossegor, **p. 85**
La Maison du Bassin,
33970 Lège-Cap-Ferret, **p. 86**
La Maison Douce,
17410 Saint-Martin-de-Ré, **p. 89**
Le Logis du Portal,
16330 Vars, **p. 91**

Centre-Auvergne

Château de la Chassagne,
23250 Saint-Hilaire-le-Château, **p. 96**
Le Chastel Montaigu,
63320 Montaigut-le-Blanc, **p. 97**
Le Manoir de La Mothe,
03450 Vicq, **p. 104**
La Villa Louise,
21420 Aloxe-Corton, **p. 103**
Le Manoir de Clénord,
41250 Mont-près-Chambord, **p. 111**
La Ferme des Foucault,
45240 Ménestreau-en-Villette, **p. 113**

West and North

Le Logis de la Cornelière,
85200 Mervent, **p. 117**
Le Château de Saint Paterne,
72610 Saint-Paterne, **p. 121**
La Seigneurie des Claies,
72430 Asnieres-sur-Vègre, **p. 122**
Le Char à bancs,
22170 Plélo, **p. 132**
Aux Pommiers de Livaye,
14340 Notre-Dame-de-Livaye, **p. 134**
La Réserve,
27620 Giverny, **p. 135**
Les Saisons,
27400 Vironvay, **p. 136**
La Gribane,
80230 Saint-Valéry-sur-Somme, **p. 137**
L'Auberge de la Grenouillère,
62170 Montreuil-sur-Mer, **p. 138**

East

Le Château d'Etoges,
51270 Étoges, **p. 142**
Le Clos du Mont d'Hor,
51220 Saint-Thierry, **p. 143**
L'Hostellerie du Château,
68420 Eguisheim, **p. 145**
Le Grand Hôtel,
88401 Gérardmer, **p. 148**
La Cholotte,
88600 Les Rouges-Eaux, **p. 149**
Les Buttes,
88310 Ventron, **p. 150**
Maison d'Hôtes de Bulgnéville,
88140 Bulgnéville, **p. 151**
Le Crêt l'Agneau,
25650 La Longeville, **p. 153**

$100–$150

Southeast

Le Mas Samarcande,
06220 Golfe-Juan-Vallauris, **p. 10**
Aux Deux Sœurs,
13210 Saint-Etienne-du-Grès, **p. 19**
La Haute Terre,
13100 Saint-Antonin-sur-Bayon, **p. 23**
Une Autre Maison,
26110 Nyons, **p. 28**
Le Chalet-hôtel de la Croix-Fry,
74230 Manigod, **p. 38**
Le Château de Saint-Maximin,
30700 Saint-Maximin, **p. 40**
La Villa Duflot,
66000 Perpignan, **p. 45**
La Signoria,
20260 Calvi, **p. 54**

Southwest

Le Chaufourg,
24400 Sourzac, **p. 64**
La Devinière,
64500 Saint-Jean-de-Luz, **p. 80**
Le Château de Maumont,
16600 Magnac-sur-Touvre, **p. 90**

Centre-Auvergne

Les Deux Abbesses,
43300 Saint-Arcons-d'Allier, **p. 100**
Le Château des Réaux,
37140 Chouzé-sur-Loire, **p. 108**
Le Domaine des Bidaudières,
37210 Vouvray, **p. 109**
Le Château de Montgouverne,
37210 Rochecorbon, **p. 110**

West and North

Lecoq-Gadby,
35700 Rennes, **p. 124**
Le Château de Guilguiffin,
29710 Landudec, **p. 128**
Le Château de Lezhildry,
22220 Plouguiel, **p. 131**

East

Les Bas-Rupts,
88400 Gérardmer, **p. 147**

$150 and up

Southeast

La Villa Estelle,
06800 Haut-de-Cagnes, **p. 13**
Hostellerie de l'Abbaye de La Celle,
83170 La Celle, **p. 16**
La Bastide de Marie,
84560 Ménerbes, **p. 26**
Les Servages,
74300 Les Carroz d'Arâches, **p. 36**
La Villa Calvi,
20260 Calvi, **p. 53**

Southwest

Le Château de la Treyne,
46200 Lacave, **p. 60**

West and North

Le Château de Noirieux,
49125 Briollay, **p. 118**
Le Château de la Ballue,
35560 Bazouges-la-Pérouse, **p. 125**
Le Château Richeux,
35350 Saint-Méloir-des-Ondes, **p. 126**

East

Chez les Colin,
25650 Montbenoît, **p. 152**

Châteaux et Hôtels de France.
Relais et Châteaux.

Art direction and layout design
Didier Gustin and Sandrine Canale

Editorial
Nicolas Rabeau and Samantha Deplanque

Maps by
Apex Cartographie

All photographs
by
Christophe Valentin